YOUR REAL-LIFE PLAYBOOK

A Student's Playbook for Money, Decisions & Adult Life

TIREMENT • TAXES • BUDGETING • CAREER • CA
JDGETING • CAREER • CARS • CREDIT CARDS • G
RS • CREDIT CARDS • GOALS • HOUSES • INVES

Austin Collins

Your Real-life Playbook: A Student's Playbook for Money, Decisions, and Adult Life

Published by Argyle Fox Publishing | argylefoxpublishing.com

ISBN 979-8-89124-297-5 (Paperback)

ISBN 979-8-89124-104-6 (Hardcover)

The information provided is for general informational and educational purposes only and should not be considered financial, legal, tax, investment, or professional advice. Any decisions made based on this information are done at your own discretion and risk. You should consult with a qualified professional such as a licensed financial advisor, attorney, or CPA before making any financial, legal, tax, or business decisions. While every effort is made to ensure accuracy, no guarantees are made regarding completeness, reliability, or applicability to your specific situation.

INTRODUCTION

Most young people leave high school academically prepared, yet fundamentally unprepared for real life. They are expected to make some of the most important decisions of their lives, such as choosing a college, taking on debt, selecting a career path, signing financial agreements, and entering the workforce without ever being taught how the systems behind those decisions actually work. The reality is that the current education system was never designed to teach everyday financial decision-making. It teaches subjects, not life outcomes.

The purpose of this curriculum is simple but powerful: to give students and parents the knowledge needed to make informed, realistic decisions about the future **before** those decisions become permanent.

The financial choices we make early in life can shape our opportunities, struggles, and freedoms for decades. Making poor financial decisions early does not mean someone can never succeed. Many people recover and go on to do very well. However, making good financial decisions early dramatically reduces unnecessary hardship and accelerates the path to financial stability and freedom.

Unfortunately, bad financial decisions can take a lifetime to undo.

Unfortunately, bad financial decisions often take years (sometimes a lifetime) to undo.

Today, Americans owe roughly **$1.8 trillion** in student loan debt. While most student loans are structured on a 10-year repayment plan, the average borrower takes **20 or more years** to pay them off and ends up paying **tens of thousands of dollars in interest** beyond what they originally borrowed. This is not because students are irresponsible. It's because they were never taught how debt, interest, repayment, taxes, and long-term trade-offs actually work together.

Topics like credit, student loans, interest rates, taxes, budgeting, insurance, investing, retirement planning, mortgages, career selection, and college cost analysis are rarely taught in school. Instead, this responsibility is often placed on parents. But many parents are still learning these lessons themselves or were never taught them at all.

As a result, most people are left with only one "education system" for real life:

trial, error, and expensive mistakes.

This curriculum exists to change that.

Through these lessons, students and parents will learn how everyday financial systems actually work—how paychecks are taxed, how to read a W-2, how tax brackets function, how debt and interest compound, how to buy a car or a home, how to budget effectively, how to plan for retirement, and how to evaluate careers and colleges through a financial lens.

What makes this program truly unique is the opportunity to apply this knowledge through a **real-world financial simulation**. Students will be able to see how their career goals, education choices, tax obligations, and lifestyle expectations play out in reality **before** committing to decisions that may follow them for decades.

So often adults say, "I wish someone had taught me this," or "If I had known this earlier, my life would look very different."

This curriculum is designed to **prevent** that **regret**.

It gives parents a structured, practical resource to guide these conversations and gives students clarity, confidence, and control over their future—not to eliminate mistakes, but to avoid unnecessary ones.

Because information doesn't guarantee perfect decisions, but lack of information almost guarantees costly ones.

Information doesn't guarantee perfect decisions, but lack of information almost guarantees costly ones.

CONTENTS

LIFE GOALS & VISION WORKSHEET • 9

STUDENT GOAL-SETTING EXERCISE • 10

HOW PAYCHECKS ARE TAXED • 14

STUDENT EXERCISE—CALCULATE TAKE-HOME PAY • 22

PARENT-GUIDED DISCUSSION • 23

CREDIT CARDS AND CARS • 24

CREDIT CARD DECISION EXERCISE • 34

PARENT-GUIDED DISCUSSION • 36

PURCHASING A CAR • 37

STUDENT EXERCISE—CAR DECISION • 49

PARENT-GUIDED DISCUSSION • 52

CAREER PATH DECISIONS • 53

STUDENT EXERCISE—COLLEGE DECISION • 67

PARENT-GUIDED DISCUSSION • 71

BUYING A HOME • 72

STUDENT EXERCISE—HOME BUYING • 85

PARENT-GUIDED DISCUSSION • 88

INVESTING & RETIREMENT • 89

STUDENT EXERCISE—INVESTING & RETIREMENT • 97

PARENT-GUIDED DISCUSSION • 100

BUDGETING • 101

FINAL REAL-LIFE BUDGET & FINANCIAL PLAN • 121

PARENT-GUIDED DISCUSSION • 126

IN CLOSING • 127

REAL-LIFE MONEY CHEAT SHEETS • 128

INDEX • 130

LIFE GOALS & VISION WORKSHEET

SETTING THE FOUNDATION FOR REAL-LIFE FINANCIAL DECISIONS

NOTE: This worksheet is designed to be completed **before** starting the rest of the curriculum.

The purpose is simple:

- To capture your dreams and goals without judgment
- To create a clear picture of the life you want
- To use these goals as a reference point throughout the curriculum

There are no right or wrong answers here. This exercise is about honesty, imagination, and clarity.

Later in this curriculum, you will build real budgets and financial scenarios that allow you to compare your goals to real-world costs and make informed decisions. This worksheet serves as the starting point for that comparison.

STUDENT GOAL-SETTING EXERCISE

PART 1: CAREER & PURPOSE

What career(s) you are interested in right now?

____

____

Why do/does this career(s) interest you?

____

____

How confident do you feel about this career choice?

☐ Very confident ☐ Somewhat confident ☐ Not sure yet

(It is completely okay to not know yet.)

PART 2: INCOME & LIFESTYLE VISION

What annual salary do you hope to earn one day? $______________ per year

What annual salary do you think you might realistically start at?

$______________ per year

How much money would you like available to spend each month after bills are paid? $______________ per month

What does having "enough money" mean to you?

____

____

____

PART 3: EDUCATION GOALS

School(s) you are considering attending:

____

____

Type of education you are considering:

☐ Community college

☐ Trade / technical school

☐ 4-year college

☐ Graduate school

☐ Unsure

Why does this option appeal to you?

____

____

____

PART 4: TRANSPORTATION GOALS

What kind of car would you like to drive one day?

____

What matters most to you in a vehicle? (Check all that apply)

☐ Reliability ☐ Appearance ☐ Other______________

☐ Brand ☐ Technology

☐ Low cost ☐ No car payment

Do you care more about the car you drive or what the car allows you to do with your money? Why?

____

PART 5: HOUSING & HOME GOALS

What type of home do you imagine owning?

☐ Apartment ☐ Townhome ☐ House ☐ Unsure

Where would you like to live? (City/state or type of area)

____

What feels more important to you right now?

☐ Size of the home

☐ Location

☐ Monthly affordability

☐ Long-term security

PART 6: QUALITY OF LIFE & FREEDOM

What does a "good life" look like to you?

____

____

____

Which of these matter most to you? (Circle your top three)

Freedom	Travel	Stability
Flexibility	Family time	Financial security

WHY THIS WORKSHEET MATTERS

This worksheet does **not** lock you into a path. It creates awareness.

As you move through the curriculum, you will repeatedly return to these answers and ask an important question:

Do my financial decisions support the life I say I want?

HOW PAYCHECKS ARE TAXED

UNDERSTANDING TAXES, PAYCHECKS, AND YOUR W-2

Before you ever spend a single dollar, taxes are taken out first.

This is one of the most misunderstood parts of adulthood and one of the biggest reasons people feel they don't make as much money as they thought they would. Many financial mistakes happen not because people earn too little, but because they misunderstand how much of their income they actually get to keep.

Before you ever spend a single dollar, taxes are taken out.

In this section, you will learn:

- How paychecks are taxed
- Why your take-home pay is lower than your salary
- How tax brackets actually work
- How to read a W-2 (one of the most important tax forms you will ever receive)

GROSS PAY VS. TAKE-HOME PAY

When you accept a job, you are usually told your salary or hourly wage. This number is called your **gross pay**.

Gross **pay** is the total amount you earn before anything is taken out.

Take-home **pay** (also called **net pay**) is the money you actually receive in your bank account after taxes and deductions.

This distinction is critical.

You cannot spend gross pay.

You can only spend take-home pay.

Many people plan their lifestyle, housing, car payments, and spending based on their gross income. This almost always leads to budgeting problems, debt, and financial stress.

WHY ARE TAXES TAKEN OUT OF YOUR PAYCHECK?

Taxes are used to fund essential public services, including:

- Roads and infrastructure
- Schools
- Emergency services
- Social Security and Medicare

Taxes are taken out automatically through a system called **withholding**. This means your employer sends a portion of your paycheck directly to the government before you ever see it.

Because this happens automatically, many people never stop to understand where their money is going until they realize they have less money than expected.

THE MAIN TYPES OF TAXES ON A PAYCHECK

Most workers will see three primary types of taxes withheld from their paychecks.

1. FEDERAL INCOME TAX

Federal income tax goes to the federal government.

- The amount you pay depends on how much you earn.
- Higher income means higher tax rates on some of your money.
- This tax uses a system called **tax brackets**, which we will explain shortly.

2. FICA TAXES (SOCIAL SECURITY & MEDICARE)

FICA taxes are flat percentages that apply to almost all workers.

- Social Security tax: **6.2%**
- Medicare tax: **1.45%**
- Total FICA tax: **7.65%**

These taxes are taken out no matter what tax bracket you are in.

3. STATE INCOME TAX (IF APPLICABLE)

Some states charge income tax, while others do not.

States with no income tax include Texas, Florida, Tennessee, and several others. If you live and work in a state with income tax, that tax will also be withheld from your paycheck.

HOW TAX BRACKETS ACTUALLY WORK (VERY IMPORTANT)

This is one of the most misunderstood topics in personal finance.

COMMON MYTH:

"If I move into a higher tax bracket, all my money gets taxed at that higher rate."

REALITY:

Only the portion of your income that falls into each bracket is taxed at that rate.

SIMPLE TAX BRACKET EXAMPLE

Imagine the following simplified tax brackets:

- 10% on the first $11,000
- 12% on income from $11,001 to $44,000
- 22% on income above $44,000

Now imagine you earn **$50,000**.

Here's how that income is taxed.

- The first $11,000 is taxed at 10%.
- The next $33,000 is taxed at 12%.
- The remaining $6,000 is taxed at 22%.

Note: Not all $50,000 is taxed at 22%, only the portion above $44,000.

This system is designed so earning more money never makes you worse off.

WHAT IS A W-2?

A **W-2** is a tax form your employer gives you every year, usually in January.

It shows:

- How much money you earned
- How much tax was taken out
- The information needed to file your taxes

You will use your W-2 when you or your parents file taxes.

HOW TO READ A W-2

You do not need to understand every box on a W-2. These are the most important ones.

BOX 1—WAGES, TIPS, OTHER COMPENSATION

This shows your taxable income.

It is often lower than your salary because certain deductions are excluded.

BOX 2—FEDERAL INCOME TAX WITHHELD

This shows how much federal income tax was taken out of your paychecks.

BOX 3—SOCIAL SECURITY WAGES

This shows the income subject to Social Security tax.

BOX 4—SOCIAL SECURITY TAX WITHHELD

This is usually 6.2% of Box 3.

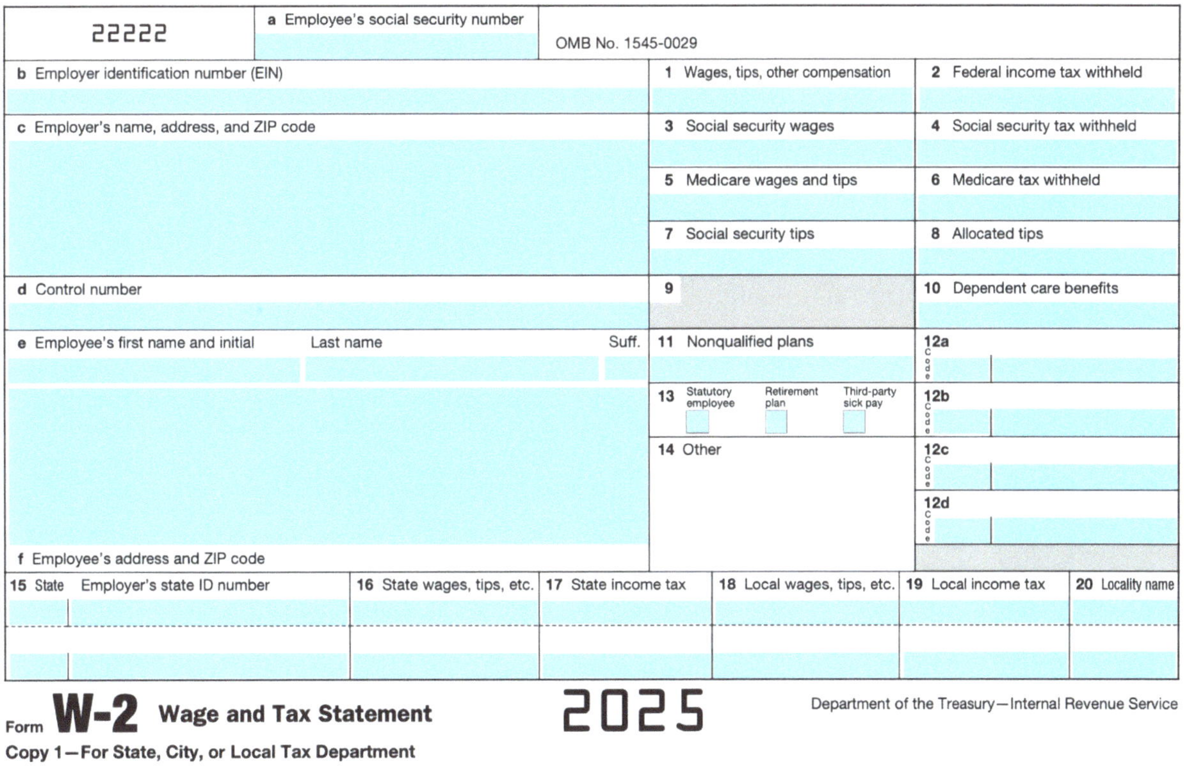

22222 | a Employee's social security number | OMB No. 1545-0029

b Employer identification number (EIN)

1 Wages, tips, other compensation | 2 Federal income tax withheld

c Employer's name, address, and ZIP code

3 Social security wages | 4 Social security tax withheld

5 Medicare wages and tips | 6 Medicare tax withheld

7 Social security tips | 8 Allocated tips

d Control number | 9 | 10 Dependent care benefits

e Employee's first name and initial | Last name | Suff. | 11 Nonqualified plans | 12a Code

13 Statutory employee | Retirement plan | Third-party sick pay | 12b Code

14 Other | 12c Code | 12d Code

f Employee's address and ZIP code

15 State | Employer's state ID number | 16 State wages, tips, etc. | 17 State income tax | 18 Local wages, tips, etc. | 19 Local income tax | 20 Locality name

Form **W-2** **Wage and Tax Statement** 2025 Department of the Treasury—Internal Revenue Service

Copy 1—For State, City, or Local Tax Department

BOX 5—MEDICARE WAGES

This shows the income subject to Medicare tax.

BOX 6—MEDICARE TAX WITHHELD

This is usually 1.45% of Box 5.

BOX 16—STATE WAGES (IF APPLICABLE)

This shows income subject to state tax.

BOX 17—STATE INCOME TAX WITHHELD

This shows how much state tax was taken out.

WHY THIS MATTERS SO MUCH

Understanding how paychecks and taxes work allows you to:

- Budget correctly
- Avoid lifestyle inflation
- Understand job offers realistically
- Avoid debt caused by overestimating income

Many people struggle financially not because they earn too little, but because they don't know how much they actually take home.

SIMPLE RULE OF THUMB FOR PLANNING

When estimating take-home pay, assume 25% of your gross income goes to taxes.

This estimate is not exact, but it is:

- Easy to remember
- Conservative
- Useful for budgeting and decision-making

Actual taxes may be lower or higher depending on income and state.

When estimating take-home pay, assume 25% of your gross income goes to taxes.

FINAL TAKEAWAYS

Your salary is not what you get to spend.

Taxes are automatic and unavoidable.

Tax brackets do not punish earning more money.

A W-2 tells the full story of your income for the year.

Budgeting must always use take-home pay.

If you can't understand your paycheck, you can't control your money.

Understanding taxes is not about becoming a tax expert. It's about making smart, realistic decisions with the money you actually have.

"If you don't understand your paycheck, you can't control your money."

STUDENT EXERCISE—CALCULATE TAKE-HOME PAY

STEP 1: INCOME

Expected annual salary: $___________

STEP 2: ESTIMATE TAXES

Choose one:

- ☐ Use actual estimate
- ☐ Use 25% rule

Note: *You can look up estimated taxes for federal and state income for your area. When you don't, remember to include Social Security and Medicare.*

Estimated taxes: $____________

STEP 3: TAKE-HOME PAY

Annual take-home pay: $__________________

Monthly take-home pay: $_________________

PARENT-GUIDED DISCUSSION

Parents and students should discuss the following together:

Does the take-home pay surprise you?

Which deductions did you not know existed?

How would budgeting change if taxes were ignored?

How does understanding take-home pay affect car, housing, and college decisions?

CREDIT CARDS AND CARS

CREDIT CARDS: HOW THEY QUIETLY DESTROY BUDGETS

Now, let's talk about two of the biggest budget destroyers for most people: **credit cards** and **cars**.

These two are responsible for blowing up more budgets than almost anything else. They are easy to access, heavily marketed, and often justified as "normal," while they quietly drain cash flow and delay financial progress for years.

We'll start with credit cards.

The reality is sobering: the average person carries between **$6,400 and $6,700** in credit-card debt. That means millions of people are not just using credit cards for convenience, but they are also carrying balances that charge high interest month after month, turning everyday purchases into long-term financial burdens.

Understanding how this happens and how to keep from falling into this trap is critical, especially early in life.

WHAT IS A CREDIT CARD?

A **credit card** is a financial tool that allows you to borrow money from a bank or credit card company to make purchases, with the agreement that you will pay the money back later.

When you use a credit card, you are not spending your own money. You are using the lender's money, and you are expected to repay it by a certain date.

HOW A CREDIT CARD WORKS (PLAIN LANGUAGE)

Simply put, here's how a credit card works.

1. The credit card company gives you a credit limit, which is the maximum amount you are allowed to borrow.
2. Each time you swipe or use the card, you are borrowing money.
3. At the end of the month, you receive a statement showing:
   - How much you borrowed
   - What you paid back
   - How much you still owe

If you pay the full balance by the due date, you usually pay no interest.

If you do not pay the full balance, the remaining amount starts accruing interest, often at very high rates.

INTEREST: WHY CREDIT CARDS ARE DANGEROUS

Interest is the extra money you pay for borrowing.

Credit cards typically charge very high interest rates, often 20% or more. This means balances can grow quickly if they are not paid off in full.

IMPORTANT DISTINCTION

A credit card is a short-term loan that becomes expensive if misused.

A credit card is:

- Not extra income
- Not free money
- Not an emergency fund

It is a **short-term loan** that becomes expensive if misused.

WHEN CREDIT CARDS CAN BE USEFUL

When used correctly, credit cards can:

- Help build credit history
- Provide short-term convenience
- Offer fraud protection
- Be useful for emergencies **only if paid off quickly**

WHEN CREDIT CARDS BECOME A PROBLEM

Credit cards become dangerous when they are:

- Used to fund a lifestyle you cannot afford
- Used to cover monthly budget shortfalls
- Paid only at the minimum payment amount
- Carried month to month with a revolving balance

This is how people slowly slide into long-term debt without realizing it.

TYPICAL INTEREST RATES ON CREDIT CARDS

Credit card interest is expressed as APR (**Annual Percentage Rate**).

Average APR range:

- Typical APR on cards with interest being charged is **~22.2% as of mid-2025**.
- Other measurements show rates at **~20%–25%** depending on the source and card type.

Important notes:

- APRs vary widely based on credit score, card type, and market conditions.
- If you only make minimum payments or carry a balance, a high APR means much of the payment goes to interest instead of reducing the amount owed (the **principal**).

AVERAGE MONTHLY PAYMENTS (CONCEPTUAL)

There is no single "official" national number for average monthly credit card payments, but we can estimate based on typical balances and repayment patterns.

Example estimate:

- Average credit card balance: **~$6,500**
- Typical minimum payment: **2–3%** of balance
- At 2%: $6,500 × 2% = **$130/month**
- At 3%: $6,500 × 3% = **$195/month**

Interest alone can be $100+ per month.

With high APR (~22%), a $130–$195 monthly payment may barely cover interest, meaning the balance barely goes down unless higher payments are made.

A real-world credit card debt study found that when the average borrower makes typical revolving payments, **interest alone can be $100+ per month** before principal is reduced.

WHAT THIS MEANS FOR YOUR BUDGET

Here's how this typically plays out for an individual:

- Balance: **~$6,500**
- APR: **~22%**
- Minimum monthly payment: **~$130–$195**

With high interest and minimum payments, it can take years to pay off a balance. In the process, it may cost thousands in interest, especially if the person continues using the card.

MINIMUM VS. INTENTIONAL PAYMENT (SIDE-BY-SIDE COMPARISON)

Strategy	Monthly Payment	Time to Pay Off	Total Paid	Interest Paid
Minimum	~$130	20+ years	~$20,000+	~$13,500+
$250/month	$250	~3 years	~$9,000	~$2,500
$400/month	$400	~18 months	~$7,200	~$700

Lesson: **The faster you attack the balance, the less power interest has.**

WHAT THIS MEANS FOR YOUR LIFE (NOT JUST YOUR BUDGET)

Credit card minimum payments steal cash flow. They crowd out:

- Saving
- Investing
- Emergency funds

Paying the minimum amount on your credit card bill creates the illusion of affordability, while quietly draining thousands of dollars over time.

This is why credit cards:

- Feel manageable in the short-term
- Become destructive in the long-term

Minimum payments are designed to keep you paying, not to get you out of debt.

THE CORE LESSON

Credit cards are not dangerous because of emergencies.

They are dangerous because:

- The damage is slow.
- The payments feel small.
- The cost is hidden.
- The time loss is massive.

If you don't control credit card debt aggressively, it will control your future quietly.

A CRITICAL REMINDER (EVEN FOR "RESPONSIBLE" USERS)

Even if you are "responsible" with a credit card and pay off the balance every month and never pay interest, that does not automatically mean the credit card is good for you or truly under your control.

The reality is that people who use credit cards consistently tend to spend more money than they would if they did not have one, even when they pay the balance in full.

This happens for a few key reasons.

1. Credit cards separate spending from the feeling of paying. With cash or debit, money leaves immediately. With credit, the pain of paying is delayed. That delay makes purchases feel smaller and less real in the moment.

2. Credit cards raise your mental spending limit. The question quietly changes from "Do I want to spend this money?" to "Can I put this on the card?"

3. Rewards and points create false incentives. Earning 1–2% back sounds appealing, but it rarely offsets the extra spending used to earn rewards.

Even disciplined users often say:

- "I'll just put it on the card and pay it off later."
- "It's fine, I get points."
- "I'll make up for it next month."

These small decisions add up quietly.

So yes, paying your card off monthly is better than carrying a balance. But if using the card causes higher spending, it still reduces how much you can save, invest, or use intentionally.

KEY LESSON

Good financial behavior is not just about avoiding interest.
It is about **controlling spending**.
If a tool causes you to spend more, even without interest,
it may still be **working against your goals**.

CREDIT CARDS IN COLLEGE: STARTING ADULT LIFE IN A HOLE

Many students get their first credit card while they are still in college. The common belief is:

"Once I graduate and get a real job, I'll pay it off."

What most students don't realize is that by doing this, they are starting adult life already in a hole they must dig out of.

While in college, most students:

- Do not have a job, or
- Earn very little money, often part-time wages

That means they are given access to a tool that allows them to charge expenses, but not the income needed to pay those charges down effectively.

When you combine:

- Low or no income
- Easy access to credit
- High interest rates

The result is almost always future financial harm.

Instead of graduating with a clean slate, many students graduate with:

- Credit card balances
- Monthly minimum payments
- Reduced cash flow on day one of their career

This puts them behind before they even start.

Credit cards in college often don't solve problems. They delay them and make them more expensive. The debt does not disappear when graduation happens. It follows you into your first job, your first apartment, and your adult budget.

What starts as a few thousand dollars can quietly become a long-term financial burden.

The average college student graduates with **$2,000–$3,000** in credit card debt. That may not sound like a lot, but when a balance is carried month to month, it can grow quickly due to high interest rates. What starts as a few thousand dollars can quietly become a long-term financial burden.

When you graduate, you are earning a starting salary, not a peak salary. At the same time, you're taking on brand-new expenses like rent, utilities, transportation, insurance, groceries, and more. Adding credit card debt on top of this makes everything harder.

Graduating with credit card debt means you are already playing catch-up before your career even begins.

Don't be the statistic. Avoid credit cards in college whenever possible. Starting adulthood debt-free gives you more freedom, more options, and a much stronger foundation.

Starting adulthood debt-free gives you more freedom, more options, and a much stronger foundation.

YEAR-BY-YEAR REALITY (MINIMUM PAYMENTS ONLY) EXAMPLE

Year	Starting Balance	Total Paid So Far	Interest Paid So Far	Balance at Year End
1	$6,500	$1,560	~$1,380	~$6,320
3	~$6,100	~$4,500	~$4,000	~$5,900
5	~$5,600	~$7,800	~$6,900	~$5,300
10	~$4,500	~$15,000	~$13,800	~$4,000
20+	$0	~$20,000+	~$13,500+	$0

VISUAL TAKEAWAY

The person above didn't buy $6,500 worth of stuff.

They bought $20,000 worth of debt slowly, quietly, and unintentionally.

This doesn't have to be you.

CREDIT CARD DECISION EXERCISE

PART 1: CREDIT CARD REALITY

Do you currently have a credit card? ☐ Yes ☐ No

If yes use your personal card or look up national averages for each:

- Current balance: $_______________
- Interest rate (APR): ______________%
- Minimum payment: $_____________

PART 2: MINIMUM PAYMENT TRAP SIMULATION

If you only pay the minimum:

- Balance: $________________
- APR: ______________%
- Estimated years to pay off:______________
- Estimated total interest paid: $_________________

PART 3: BEHAVIOR CHECK

What is the card mostly used for?

☐ Emergencies ☐ Convenience ☐ Lifestyle spending ☐ Bills

Would you spend the same amount if you used cash or debit?

☐ Yes ☐ No ☐ Not sure

PART 4: BUDGET IMPACT

Monthly take-home pay: $________________

Credit card payment: $_____________

What could this payment fund instead?

☐ Savings ☐ Investing ☐ Debt freedom ☐ Stress reduction

PART 5: RISK REFLECTION

If you lost income for 3 months, could you still pay this? ☐ Yes ☐ No

Does this card increase or reduce financial stress? ☐ Increase ☐ Reduce

STUDENT FINAL REFLECTION

Is a credit card helping you or hurting you right now? ☐ Helping ☐ Hurting ☐ Unsure

Should credit cards be used without stable income? ☐ Yes ☐ No

PARENT-GUIDED DISCUSSION

Parents and students should discuss the following together.

Why do credit cards feel easier than cash?

How does interest change the cost of purchases?

What habits lead to balances growing?

Is credit history worth the risk of debt?

What alternatives exist for emergencies?

PURCHASING A CAR

ONE OF THE MOST IMPORTANT (AND REPEATED) FINANCIAL DECISIONS OF YOUR LIFE

Now let's move on to what is probably the single most damaging financial decision people make over and over again throughout their lifetime:

purchasing a car.

Cars are one of the most common purchases people make to:

- Look successful
- Feel cool or accomplished
- Feel good about themselves

But the reality is that car purchases cause more financial stress and failure than almost any other expense. Many families and individuals become **car poor**.

WHAT DOES "CAR POOR" MEAN?

Being car poor means:

- You pay so much each month for a car that very little money is left after bills.
- You constantly have to watch every dollar just to survive.
- You fall behind on other bills.
- You rely on credit cards or loans to cover gaps in your income.

Eventually, many people in this situation:

- Accumulate more debt
- Miss payments
- Have their vehicle repossessed

When that happens, all the money they paid is gone, with **nothing** to show for it.

WHY CARS ARE SO DANGEROUS FINANCIALLY

Cars are easy to get approved for. In fact, cars are one of the easiest things to finance.

Many dealerships will approve buyers:

- With bad credit
- With no credit
- With very little income

This makes cars feel affordable even when they are not.

Cars are one of the easiest things to finance.

WHAT IS CREDIT?

Credit is your ability to borrow money with the promise that you will pay it back later. Lenders decide whether to lend to you (and at what interest rate) based on your **credit score**.

WHAT IS A CREDIT SCORE?

A **credit score** is a number that represents how risky it is to lend you money.

It is based on things like:

- Whether you pay bills on time
- How much debt you have
- How long you've had credit
- How often you apply for credit

Important notes for students:

- If you have bad credit, you usually get high interest rates.
- If you have no credit, you are still considered risky.
- High interest means a higher monthly payment.
- High interest means a higher total cost.

WHY NEW CARS ARE ESPECIALLY RISKY

Many people want a new car because:

- Dealers may offer lower interest rates
- New cars come with warranties
- They look nicer and feel more reliable

But new cars come with a major financial problem: **depreciation**.

WHAT IS A DEPRECIATING ASSET?

A **depreciating asset** is something that loses value over time.

A car is a depreciating asset. That means:

- It will not make you money
- It is worth less every year
- Every mile driven reduces its value

Cars, boats, campers, ATVs, and similar items are not investments. You may use a vehicle for work or business, but the vehicle itself is not the investment.

IMMEDIATE DEPRECIATION (THE HIDDEN LOSS)

Most new vehicles lose **$5,000–$10,000** in value immediately when driven off the lot.

The moment you drive away:

- The car is now considered "used."
- The value drops instantly.

This leads to a dangerous situation.

WHAT DOES "BEING UPSIDE DOWN" MEAN?

Being upside down (or underwater) on a car means you owe more money on the loan than the car is worth.

This often happens almost immediately with new vehicles.

WHAT IS EQUITY?

Equity is the difference between what something is worth and what you owe on it.

- **Positive equity:** The car is worth more than you owe.
- **Negative equity:** You owe more than the car is worth.

THE TRADE-IN TRAP (WHERE IT GETS UGLY)

Three years after driving away with a new car, a person wants a different car. The dealer says: **"No problem. We'll roll your balance into the new loan."**

However, there is a problem. A big one.

What actually happens:

- The negative equity from the old car is added to the new car loan.
- Now you are paying for two cars wrapped into one.

This creates:

- A very high loan balance
- A very high monthly payment

Most people can't afford the payment, so they do the next worst thing.

LONGER LOANS MAKE IT WORSE

To lower the monthly payment, many people:

- Finance the car for longer terms
- 5 years becomes 6, 7, or even 8 years

This:

- Keeps them in debt longer
- Increases total interest paid
- Almost guarantees they stay upside down

This creates a debt snowball that takes years or even decades to escape.

THE WORST PART

Even if the car breaks down, the warranty expires, and the car becomes unreliable, you still owe the money. This is how people become financially imprisoned by car payments.

WHAT STUDENTS SHOULD DO INSTEAD

If you are responsible for purchasing your own vehicle, never start with a new car. Instead, remember:

- Your car's job is to get you from Point A to Point B.
- Older vehicles can do this just as well.
- Used vehicles can still have warranties.
- Many dealerships offer warranties on used cars.

THE BEST CAR STRATEGY

- Buy a car in cash if possible.
- Buy what you can afford, not what you qualify for.
- If financing is necessary:
  - Finance as little as possible
  - Finance for less than 5 years
  - Never finance longer than 5 years

But remember: the goal is always to avoid debt, especially on depreciating assets.

FINAL RULE (VERY IMPORTANT)

Never think: **"What monthly payment can I afford?"**

Always think: **"What can I afford out of pocket?"**

A car payment you don't have is one of the most freeing financial advantages you can have early in life.

Later in this curriculum, you will see how avoiding even small amounts of car debt can be worth hundreds of thousands or even millions of dollars over time.

REALISTIC COST EXAMPLE: BUYING A NEW CAR (~$20,000)

Scenario: You decide to buy a new car priced at $20,000.

To make this clear and conservative, we'll assume:

- You put $0 down (you borrow the full $20,000)
- Interest rate: 7% APR
- Loan term options we'll compare:
  - 48 months (4 years)
  - 60 months (5 years)
  - 72 months (6 years — dangerous)

OPTION 1—48-MONTH LOAN (4-YEAR TERM)

Loan: $20,000

Interest rate: 7%

Monthly payment: ~$476

Total paid: $476 × 48 = $22,848

Total interest paid: ~$2,848

OPTION 2—60-MONTH LOAN (5-YEAR TERM)

Loan: $20,000

Interest rate: 7%

Monthly payment: ~$396

Total paid: $396 × 60 = $23,760

Total interest paid: ~$3,760

OPTION 3—72-MONTH LOAN (6-YEAR TERM)

Loan: $20,000

Interest rate: 7%

Monthly payment: ~$336

Total paid: $336 × 72 = $24,192

Total interest paid: ~$4,192

COMPARISON—NEW CAR AT $20,000

Term	Monthly Payment	Total Paid	Interest Paid	Years Owing
48 mo	$476	$22,848	$2,848	4
60 mo	$396	$23,760	$3,760	5
72 mo	$336	$24,192	$4,192	6

KEY INSIGHTS FOR STUDENTS

One of the most important lessons in car financing is this: **Longer loans always cost more**, even when the monthly payment looks easier to manage.

As loan terms increase, the monthly payment goes down but the **total interest paid goes up**. Using this example:

- **4-year loan: ~$2,848** in interest
- **5-year loan: ~$3,760** in interest
- **6-year loan: ~$4,192** in interest

By choosing a **6-year loan instead of a 4-year loan**, you pay about **$1,344 more** in interest for the same vehicle.

Longer loans also keep you in debt for more years, which creates additional problems, which include:

- You're still making payments after the car has lost a large portion of its value.
- You may owe money when the car becomes unreliable or breaks down.
- You delay saving and investing during critical early years.

WHY THIS MATTERS EVEN MORE: DEPRECIATION

At the same time interest is working against you, **depreciation** is also quietly reducing the value of the vehicle.

A new car typically **loses 20–30% of its value in the first year alone**, simply because it is no longer considered new once it leaves the dealership. From there, depreciation continues every year as the car accumulates miles, experiences wear and tear, and becomes less desirable in the used market.

By **five years of age**, most cars are worth only **40–50% of their original price**. For a **$20,000 new car**, that often means a value of just **$8,000 to $10,000** after five years.

In practical terms, **$10,000 to $12,000 of value has disappeared**, even if the car is in good condition and fully paid off. This loss does not include interest, insurance, fuel, maintenance, repairs, or registration. It is purely the decline in value of the vehicle itself.

In this example, after five years you paid **$23,760 for a $20,000 car** that may only be worth **$8,000–$10,000** by the time the loan is finished.

This is why cars are considered **depreciating assets**. They provide transportation and convenience, but they do not build wealth. The loss does not happen only when the car is sold. **It happens gradually every day the vehicle is owned**, starting the moment it is purchased.

THE REAL COST (THE MOST IMPORTANT POINT)

Let's revisit the **5-year (60-month) loan**.

- You make payments for **60 months**.
- You pay **$3,760 in interest**.
- The car may be worth **half of its original value** when the loan ends.

Because the car was financed:

- Money was lost to **interest**.
- Money was lost to **depreciation**.
- **No wealth was built** with that money.

That last point is the most important takeaway in this entire section.

No wealth is built with money lost to interest or depreciation.

This is not about saying people should never buy a nice car. There is nothing wrong with owning something you enjoy. The problem is **timing**. Buying expensive, financed vehicles early in life — before financial stability is established — is one of the biggest wealth killers there is.

The most common mistake people make is this:

Just because you can afford the monthly payment does not mean you can afford the car.

In this example, the payment is roughly **$400 per month**. On the surface, that doesn't feel extreme. But that $400 is not just a car payment — it is **lost opportunity**.

That same $400 per month could have been:

- Earning returns
- Compounding over time
- Growing into real assets

Instead, it is being sent to:

- Interest
- Depreciation
- A vehicle that loses value every day

You are not just losing $400 per month. You are potentially losing **hundreds of thousands — even millions — of dollars over your lifetime** because that money is no longer working for you through compounding growth.

Later in this curriculum, you will see exactly what that $400 per month becomes when it is invested instead — and how small decisions made early in life create massive consequences decades later.

THE CORE LESSON

Build wealth first. Buy nice things later.

Debt-building tools create the illusion of success.

Wealth-building tools create real freedom.

This is why cars are financially dangerous. They quietly steal the most powerful years of compounding when you can least afford to lose them.

IF YOU MUST BORROW: A SAFE RULE TO LIVE BY

THE 20/3/8 RULE (VERY COMMON, VERY SAFE)

This rule is designed to keep a car from destroying your cash flow.

1. 20% down payment. Put at least 20% down to reduce interest, avoid being upside down, and lower risk.

2. 3-year loan maximum (36 months). Shorter loans reduce total interest and force you to buy less car.

3. 8% of gross monthly income max. Your total car costs should not exceed 8% of your gross monthly income. This includes your car payment and insurance.

If you can't meet the 20/3/8 rule, the car is too expensive.

CAR PAYMENT REALITY (RECENT STATISTICS)

According to recent data, the average monthly auto loan payment in the U.S. is approximately:

- **$748–$749** per month for new vehicles
- **$529–$532** per month for used vehicles

Average loan amounts:

- New cars: **~$41,983** financed on average
- Used cars: **~$26,795** financed on average

Don't be one of these statistics. Buy what you can afford and imagine what this money could be used for instead.

STUDENT EXERCISE—CAR DECISION

PART 1: TRANSPORTATION NEEDS (NOT WANTS)

Primary purpose of vehicle: ☐ School ☐ Work ☐ Both ☐ Other: ______________

Miles driven per year (estimate): ______________

Is reliability more important than appearance? ☐ Yes ☐ No

PART 2: CAR OPTION COMPARISON

Option A: New or Expensive Vehicle

- Vehicle price: $___________
- Down payment: $______________
- Loan amount: $___________
- Interest rate (APR): _____________%
- Loan term (months): ____________

  Estimated monthly payment: $______________

  Estimated total paid over loan: $_____________

Option B: Used / Modest Vehicle

- Vehicle price: $___________
- Down payment / cash purchase: $_____________
- Loan amount: $___________
- Interest rate (APR):_____________%
- Loan term (months): ____________

  Estimated monthly payment: $______________

  Estimated total paid over loan: $_____________

PART 3: CAR AFFORDABILITY RULES CHECK

Expected annual salary: $____________

- 35% salary car value limit: $____________
- 50% salary car value limit (max): $____________

Does Option A follow the rule? ☐ Yes ☐ No

Does Option B follow the rule? ☐ Yes ☐ No

PART 4: MONTHLY BUDGET IMPACT

Monthly take-home pay: $____________

- Car payment: $____________
- Insurance: $____________
- Gas: $____________
- Maintenance: $____________

Total monthly car cost: $____________

What % of take-home pay is this?____________%

☐ Under 10% (Good) ☐ 10–15% (Caution) ☐ Over 15% (High Risk)

PART 5: OPPORTUNITY COST REFLECTION

If this car payment did not exist, where could that money go?

☐ Savings ☐ Investing ☐ Emergency fund ☐ Housing ☐ Flexibility

Explain: ____

____

____

STUDENT FINAL REFLECTION

Does this car help or hurt your future? ☐ Helps ☐ Hurts ☐ Depends on choice

If you could not afford this car in cash, should you buy it? ☐ Yes ☐ No

PARENT-GUIDED DISCUSSION

Is the car serving a need or a status image?

How does the payment affect savings and stress?

What happens if income drops?

What would a cheaper car make possible?

How does delaying a nice car benefit long-term wealth?

CAREER PATH DECISIONS

COLLEGE, TRADE, TECHNICAL SCHOOL, OR SOMETHING ELSE?

One of the biggest questions we are asked early in life is:

"What do you want to do for a career?"

For some people, the answer comes quickly. For others, it takes years. But whether someone knows exactly what they want to do or has no idea at all, most students hear the same message from parents, teachers, counselors, friends, or online advice:

"You need to go to college to be successful."

Because of this message, many students don't see college as one option. They see it as the only option. So instead of asking what path fits best, the first questions become:

- What school should I go to?
- What school sounds exciting?
- What school looks prestigious?
- Where do my friends want to go?
- What is my "dream school"?

Very few students are taught to ask the most important question first:

Can I afford this path, and does it make financial sense for my future?

HOW MOST STUDENTS CHOOSE A COLLEGE (AND WHY THAT'S RISKY)

Many students choose a school based on:

- Campus life and social scene
- Distance from home
- Friends or family attending

- Sports teams and reputation
- Prestige or "status"
- A dream school they've imagined for years

What often gets ignored:

- Total cost of attendance
- How much debt will be required
- What monthly payments will look like after graduation
- Whether the expected salary supports the debt

This disconnect is one of the main reasons student loan debt has become such a large problem.

THE REALITY OF STUDENT LOAN DEBT

Today, Americans owe roughly **$1.8 trillion** in student loans.

Most student loans are designed to be paid back over **10 years**, but in reality:

- The average borrower often takes **20+ years**.
- Many pay **tens of thousands of dollars** in interest.
- Some feel financially stuck even with a good job.

To understand why, students need to understand how loans actually work.

Even if you drop out of college and never earn a degree, you must pay back any loans you take out.

KEY FINANCIAL TERMS (EXPLAINED SIMPLY)

Principal. The amount of money you originally borrow.

Interest. The extra money you pay for borrowing. This is the cost of the loan.

Repayment plan. The rules that determine:

- How much you pay each month
- How long you stay in debt
- How much you pay total

Take-home pay. The money you actually receive after taxes are taken out of your paycheck.

COLLEGE COMPLETION RISK (OFTEN IGNORED)

Another major risk students rarely think about is not finishing college. However, it is a reality for many.

- Roughly **35–40%** of students who start a bachelor's degree do not finish within **6–8 years** or at all.
- Nearly **1 in 3** never earn the degree they originally pursued.
- Many drop out within the first year.

If you leave college early:

- You still owe the debt.
- You may not have a degree.
- You often earn less income.
- Repayment becomes much harder.

This creates one of the most difficult financial situations a young adult can face.

THE CORE FINANCIAL PROBLEM

Most people struggling with student loans fall into one of these groups:

- They were pushed into college without exploring alternatives.
- They chose a school they couldn't afford.
- They overpaid for a degree relative to income.
- They borrowed without understanding repayment.
- They finished school, but the salary didn't justify the cost.

This is not a failure of intelligence or effort.

It is a failure of financial education before decisions are made.

INCOME-TO-DEBT RATIO (A CRITICAL CONCEPT)

Income-to-debt ratio compares how much you earn to how much you owe.

If debt is too large compared to income:

- Monthly payments control your life.
- Saving becomes difficult.
- Investing gets delayed.
- Stress increases.
- Choices shrink.

This concept applies to student loans, cars, homes, and credit cards.

TWO RULES THAT PROTECT STUDENTS FROM OVERPAYING

RULE 1: THE 1× STARTING SALARY RULE

Your total student loan debt at graduation should not exceed your expected first-year salary. Example:

- Starting salary: **$60,000**
- Maximum debt: **$60,000**

This is a good basic rule, but there is a safer one.

RULE 2: THE 75% STARTING SALARY RULE

Your total student loan debt at graduation should be no more than 75% of your expected first-year salary. Example:

- Starting salary: **$60,000**
- 75% maximum debt: **$45,000**

This rule leaves room for:

- Rent
- Transportation
- Food
- Taxes
- Emergency savings
- Retirement investing

WHY STUDENT LOAN REPAYMENT PLANS MATTER

Student loans are not all repaid the same way. Borrowers end up in different repayment plans depending on whether they can afford the payment.

Standard Repayment (10-Year Fixed)

- Same payment every month
- Loan paid off in 10 years
- Lowest total interest cost
- Only works if the payment fits your budget

Income-Driven Repayment (IDR)

- Payment based mostly on income
- Repayment lasts 20–25 years
- Much higher total cost
- Often used because the standard plan is unaffordable

Lower monthly payments feel safer but usually cost far more over time.

REAL-LIFE SIMULATION: SAME PERSON, DIFFERENT DECISIONS

Assumptions Used in All Examples

- Starting salary: **$60,000**
- Estimated take-home pay: **~$3,750/month**
- Basic living expenses: **~$2,650/month**
- Money available before loans: **~$1,100/month**
- Investment return assumption: **8%**
- Comparison age: **42** (20 years after graduation)

Path	Breaks Rule	Breaks Rule	Follows Rule	Zero Debt
Total Debt	$120,000	$120,000	$45,000	$0
Repayment Plan	Standard (10-year)	Income-driven	Standard (10-year)	None
Monthly Payment	~$1,330	~$700	~$500	$0
Years in Repay	10	25	10	0
Total Paid on Loans	~$160,000	~$210,000	~$60,000	$0
Interest Paid	~$40,000	~$90,000	~$15,000	$0
Monthly Invest. Cash	Not feasible	~$400	~$600	~$1,100
Invest. Value at 42	$0	~$235,000	~$353,000	~$647,000
NET Wealth at 42	$0	~$25,000	~$293,000	~$647,000

WHAT THIS TABLE SHOWS CLEARLY

Income-driven repayment:

- Lasts **15 years longer** than the standard plan
- Costs **$150,000 more** than borrowing responsibly
- Leaves the borrower with almost **no real wealth after 20 years**

The biggest loss shown on this chart is not interest. It is **lost compounding time**.

**Same person.
Same income.
Different decisions.**

NEVER MAKE FINANCIAL DECISIONS BASED ON ASSUMPTIONS

Do not choose debt based on what you think you might earn someday or on the highest salary you believe you could reach in your career. Future income is never guaranteed. Promotions get delayed, industries change, jobs disappear, and life happens. The income you expect later may never come.

Always evaluate debt based on the **lowest realistic income** you will earn, not the best-case scenario.

Every career starts at the bottom. If you cannot afford a debt payment at your starting or low-income level, you may never reach your higher-earning years. Heavy debt can limit your choices, force you into jobs you don't want, prevent you from taking opportunities, and in extreme cases push you into bankruptcy or long-term financial hardship.

Debt should never be justified by thoughts, such as:

- "I'll make more money later."
- "Once I get promoted, it will be fine."
- "At the peak of my career, this won't matter."

Those assumptions are how people become financially trapped.

Lifestyle Consequences

Because of debt, many:

- Can't buy a home
- Delay marriage or kids
- Can't take career risks
- Can't go back to school
- Get stuck in jobs they don't like
- Live paycheck to paycheck despite a "good" salary

This is what people mean by "golden handcuffs."

Instead of making the assumptions above, ask yourself this question:

Can I comfortably afford this payment at my lowest expected income?

If the answer is no, the debt is too large, no matter how promising the future seems. Build your financial decisions on certainty, not hope.

Hope does not pay bills. Income does.

This mindset protects you early in life, keeps your options open, and gives you the freedom to actually reach higher earning levels instead of being buried by debt before you ever get there.

You will see this repeatedly: **the goal is always no debt.**

A CRITICAL NOTE ABOUT GRADUATE SCHOOL

An important point to understand is that everything we have discussed so far applies to graduate school as well.

If you pursue a master's degree or doctorate, the key question is still the same:

What will your starting salary be when you graduate?

This is where many people get into serious trouble.

A common belief is that more education automatically equals more money. In reality, this is often not true. Many people earn a master's degree only to make the same salary they could have earned with a bachelor's degree. In some cases, there is little to no financial return at all.

To make matters worse, graduate programs often cost as much or more than undergraduate degrees, depending on the field. This means people can spend significantly more money without increasing their earning power.

There are careers where advanced degrees are required. Examples include becoming doctors, lawyers, or other specialists. However, even in those cases, the same financial rules still apply. Doctors may earn high incomes, but many make poor education and borrowing decisions along the way and end up financially strapped for years, sometimes decades. They earn a lot of money on paper, but don't get to enjoy it until much later in life because of overwhelming debt.

RESEARCH THE DEGREE, NOT JUST THE SCHOOL

One very important rule:

Not all degrees are valuable.

Not all degrees are valuable.

There are many degrees offered by colleges that:

- Cost a lot of money
- Have little demand in the job market
- Do not lead to meaningful income

Having a degree by itself does not earn you money. A degree only has value if it is valuable to:

- Employers
- Businesses
- Clients
- A specific service or skill set

Do not go to college or pursue a degree simply to say you have one. That can easily become one of the most expensive mistakes you ever make.

A degree is a tool, not a guarantee.

THE BEST-CASE SCENARIO

The best financial outcome is always graduating with NO student debt.

Do your best to:

- Earn a full scholarship
- Attend a school covered by grants

- Use a state-sponsored, free community college program
- Have parents help cover costs at a lower-priced school

If you can do any or all of the above, those options should be seriously prioritized.

The guidelines discussed earlier are **debt ceilings**, not **debt goals**. Just because a certain amount of debt is considered "manageable" does not mean you should aim for it.

Less debt is always better.

PRACTICAL, LOWER-RISK PATHS

There is nothing wrong with:

- Attending community college for two years
- Transferring to finish a four-year degree
- Taking time to explore interests at a lower cost

Many states offer free or very low-cost community college programs, which can dramatically reduce your risk. If you are unsure what career you want to pursue, this approach allows you to explore options without paying premium prices for uncertainty.

KEY TAKEAWAYS

- More education does not automatically mean more income
- Graduate school should be evaluated just like undergraduate school
- Always compare total cost vs starting salary
- Avoid debt whenever possible
- Debt limits are not targets
- The goal is flexibility, freedom, and options

Education should open doors, not create financial chains.

COLLEGE IS NOT THE ONLY PATH TO SUCCESS

College is one path, not the path.

The reality is that college isn't for everyone. Instead of forcing yourself down a path you're not interested in, it's important to understand that there are other options. In many cases, there are better options.

Success doesn't come from following the most common path. It comes from choosing the path that fits your skills, interests, and goals, and what makes sense financially. College can be a great choice when it aligns with those things, but it is not the only way to build a successful, stable, and fulfilling life.

Many high-paying, in-demand careers do not require a four-year degree and often make entrepreneurship easier.

Avoiding student debt allows people to:

- Earn sooner
- Save earlier
- Take career risks
- Start businesses faster

HIGH-PAYING PATHS THAT DO NOT REQUIRE A 4-YEAR DEGREE

Skilled Trades

Electrician, plumber, HVAC, welder, carpenter, mechanic

- $70k–$100k+ experienced
- $120k–$250k+ business owners

Trade & Technical Schools (1–2 Years)

Automation, robotics, CNC, maintenance

- $50k–$100k+

Tech (Skills > Degrees)

IT, cybersecurity, development

- $60k–$120k+

License-Based Careers

Real estate, insurance, trucking, inspection

- $50k–$150k+

Service Businesses

Landscaping, pressure washing, cleaning, painting

- $75k–$200k+ owners

WHY TRADES & LICENSING MAKE BUSINESS OWNERSHIP EASIER

- Skills solve real problems.
- Customers pay quickly.
- Demand is local and recurring.
- Pricing is straightforward.
- Income scales with effort and ownership.

Many people become financially successful not by avoiding learning — but by choosing paths where their skills are valuable without massive debt.

FINAL LESSON

The goal is not college. The goal is choosing a path that creates a strong return on your time, money, and effort.

No matter which path you choose, the primary goal should always be the same: **avoid debt whenever possible, especially student loan debt**. Debt limits your choices, delays your progress, and makes life more stressful than it needs to be. Student debt is particularly dangerous because it often lasts for decades and cannot easily be removed, even in financial hardship.

Before taking on any student loans, you should explore every option available:

- Scholarships and grants
- Community college and transfer programs
- In-state and lower-cost schools
- Trade and technical schools
- Licensing and certification programs
- Apprenticeships and paid training
- Entering the workforce sooner and gaining experience

Choose the path that creates the least financial burden, not the one that sounds the most impressive.

If student loans are absolutely necessary, remember the rules discussed in this curriculum, but understand what they truly are. The starting salary rules are **debt ceilings**, not **debt goals**. They represent the maximum amount of debt that may be manageable, not what you should aim for.

The ideal outcome is always the same:

Graduate with as little debt as possible and zero debt whenever it can be achieved.

The less debt you have, the more freedom you gain.

- Freedom to save and invest early
- Freedom to change careers or take opportunities
- Freedom from long-term financial stress
- Freedom to build wealth instead of paying interest

The goal is not to manage debt well.

The goal is to avoid it whenever possible.

That single mindset will shape your financial future more than almost any other decision you make.

STUDENT EXERCISE—COLLEGE DECISION

This exercise is designed to help students and parents make intentional, realistic college decisions instead of emotional or assumption-based ones. The goal is not to push college or discourage it, but rather to understand cost vs. outcome.

PART 1: CAREER DIRECTION (BEST GUESS. IT'S OKAY TO CHANGE LATER.)

Career(s) you are considering: ______________________________

____

Why does this career interest you?

____

____

Expected starting salary for this career (conservative estimate): $________ /year

Expected highest realistic salary later in career (optional): $________ /year

PART 2: COLLEGE OPTIONS COMPARISON

List up to three realistic college options you are considering.

School Option 1

School name: ______________________

- Tuition & fees (per year): $______________
- Room & board (per year): $______________
- Books & misc (per year): $______________
- Scholarships / grants: –$______________

  Total annual cost: $______________

  Total 4-year cost: $______________

School Option 2

School name: ______________________________

- Tuition & fees (per year): $__________________
- Room & board (per year): $__________________
- Books & misc (per year): $__________________
- Scholarships / grants: –$__________________

Total annual cost: $__________________

Total 4-year cost: $__________________

School Option 3

School name: ______________________________

- Tuition & fees (per year): $__________________
- Room & board (per year): $__________________
- Books & misc (per year): $__________________
- Scholarships / grants: –$__________________

Total annual cost: $__________________

Total 4-year cost: $__________________

PART 3: HOW WILL THIS BE PAID FOR?

For your top choice school, estimate how costs will be covered.

- Scholarships / grants: $____________
- Parent contribution: $____________
- Your savings / work: $____________
- Student loans needed: $____________

PART 4: DEBT REALITY CHECK (VERY IMPORTANT)

Expected starting salary: $________________________

Apply the rules:

- 100% salary rule (max debt): $________________________
- 75% salary rule (safer max): $________________________

Actual student loan amount needed: $____________________

☐ Below 75% (Good)

☐ Between 75%–100% (Caution)

☐ Above 100% (High Risk)

PART 5: MONTHLY PAYMENT REALITY

Estimated student loan amount: $________________________

Estimated monthly payment (10-year repayment): $________________________

Does this payment feel affordable at your starting salary? ☐ Yes ☐ No ☐ Not sure

PART 6: LIFESTYLE IMPACT REFLECTION

If you had this loan payment, which of the following might be affected? (Check all that apply).

☐ Housing choices ☐ Car choices ☐ Saving & investing

☐ Stress level ☐ Ability to change careers ☐ Ability to move

Explain (continued on next page):____

____

____

PART 7: ALTERNATIVES EXPLORATION

If the above options feel risky, what alternatives interest you?

- ☐ Community college + transfer
- ☐ In-state school
- ☐ Scholarships search
- ☐ Trade / technical school
- ☐ Delaying college
- ☐ Working while attending school

Which alternative could reduce debt the most?______________________

____

____

STUDENT FINAL REFLECTION

What surprised you most during this exercise?______________________

____

If this were your real money, would you still make the same choice?

☐ Yes ☐ No ☐ Unsure

PARENT-GUIDED DISCUSSION

Parents should listen more than talk during this section.

The goal is guidance, not pressure.

What career paths feel realistic right now, and why?

How does the cost of each school compare to starting salary?

Does the debt required feel manageable at the lowest income level?

What trade-offs would debt force in early adulthood?

Are there lower-cost paths that lead to the same outcome?

How important is the school name versus skills and experience?

BUYING A HOME

UNDERSTANDING MORTGAGES, HOMEOWNERSHIP, AND LONG-TERM WEALTH

For generations, **homeownership has been considered the American Dream**. Not because homes are flashy or exciting, but because owning a home has historically been one of the most powerful ways to build **wealth, stability, and long-term freedom**.

A home is often the largest purchase you will ever make, and it can either:

- Become your greatest wealth-building tool, or
- Turn into a financial burden that keeps you stressed and stuck

The difference comes down to timing, debt, discipline, and understanding the process.

If you enter your first career with minimal debt, homeownership becomes far easier and more attainable than for someone buried in student loans, car payments, and credit card debt. Debt reduces how much you can borrow, raises your interest rate, and limits your choices before you ever begin house shopping.

This section explains how homeownership actually works, not the version you see on social media.

WHAT IS A MORTGAGE?

A **mortgage** is a loan used to purchase a home.

Most people do not buy homes with cash. Instead, they:

1. **Borrow money** from a bank or lender

2. **Agree to repay it over time**, usually 15–30 years
3. **Pay interest** for the use of that money

Each monthly mortgage payment typically includes:

- **Principal**—the amount you borrowed
- **Interest**—the cost of borrowing
- **Property taxes**
- **Homeowners insurance**

This combination is commonly referred to as **PITI**.

WHAT IS AN ASSET?

An **asset** is something you own that has value and can help build wealth.

A home is considered an asset because:

- It **typically increases in value** over time
- It **builds equity**
- It provides **housing stability**
- It can eventually be **owned outright**

Home values have historically appreciated over time.

Unlike cars, which depreciate, homes have historically **appreciated over long periods of time**.

WHY A HOME IS ONE OF THE BEST WEALTH-BUILDING ASSETS

A primary residence is unique because:

- You are paying for housing anyway
- Each payment can **increase ownership**
- **Inflation works in your favor**
- **A paid-off home dramatically reduces expenses**

Over time, mortgage payments stay relatively stable, while **rent usually increases**.

WHAT IS HOME EQUITY?

Equity is the portion of the home you truly own.

Equity = Home value – Mortgage balance

You build equity by:

- Paying down the mortgage
- The home increasing in value

Equity matters because it:

- Increases **net worth**
- Provides **financial security**
- Represents **ownership, not debt**
- Can be used strategically later *(with caution)*

THE GOAL: NEVER BE HOUSE POOR

Being **house poor** means too much of your income goes toward housing. Common signs include:

- Little money left after bills
- No ability to save or invest
- Stress over repairs or emergencies
- Relying on credit cards to survive

A house should support your life, not control it.

WHAT IS A HEALTHY MORTGAGE PAYMENT?

A healthy rule of thumb:

Total housing costs should be no more than 25–30% of take-home pay.

This includes:

- Mortgage
- Property taxes
- Insurance
- HOA fees

Just because a bank approves you for more does not mean you should spend more.

MORTGAGE INTEREST RATES

The **interest rate** is the cost of borrowing money.

Interest rates are affected by:

- The economy
- Inflation
- **Your credit score**
- Your **debt-to-income ratio**

Lower debt + better credit = lower interest rates

Even a small rate difference can cost **tens or hundreds of thousands** of dollars over the life of a loan.

WHY CREDIT SCORE MATTERS SO MUCH

Your **credit score** signals how risky you are as a borrower.

A higher score generally means:

- Lower interest rate
- Lower monthly payment
- Better loan options

High debt from **credit cards, car loans, and student loans** lowers your score and limits your ability to buy a home affordably.

SHOPPING MORTGAGE RATES (VERY IMPORTANT)

You should **always shop mortgage rates**.

Different lenders can offer:

- Different interest rates
- Different fees
- Different loan structures

Shopping rates can save thousands without changing the house you buy.

TYPES OF MORTGAGE LOANS (BASIC OVERVIEW)

- **Conventional loans**—most common, good credit required
- **FHA loans**—lower down payment, higher fees
- **VA loans**—for eligible veterans, often no down payment, high fees
- **USDA loans**—rural areas, income limits

Each loan type has pros and cons depending on your situation.

DOWN PAYMENTS

A **down payment** is money paid upfront.

Common ranges include:

- 3–5%—low down payment programs
- 10–20%—stronger position
- 20%+ —avoids extra insurance costs

Larger down payments mean:

- Lower monthly payment
- Less interest paid
- More equity immediately

PROPERTY TAXES, INSURANCE, AND HOAS

Ongoing housing costs include:

- **Property taxes**
- **Homeowners insurance**
- **HOA fees** (if applicable)

These costs are **real, recurring, and must be budgeted**.

THE HOME BUYING PROCESS (STEP BY STEP)

Buying a home is **not a single decision**. It is a process made up of several smaller decisions, each one building on the last. When done in the right order, homeownership can become a powerful wealth-building tool. When rushed or misunderstood, it can quickly turn into financial stress.

Understanding the process ahead of time gives you control instead of pressure.

1. ASSESS YOUR FINANCES

Before looking at homes or talking to lenders, you must understand what you can realistically afford.

This step is about your **financial foundation**, not your dream house.

You should review your take-home pay (not your salary), existing debt, monthly expenses, emergency savings, and money set aside for a down payment. This is also where the **25–30% housing rule** matters most. A healthy housing payment, which includes mortgage, taxes, insurance, and HOA fees, should generally stay within 25–30% of your take-home pay.

This rule protects your future. It ensures you can still save, invest, handle repairs, and enjoy life without becoming house poor.

The key question at this stage is not "What house do I want?"

It is "**What payment supports my life long-term?**"

2. GET PRE-APPROVED

Getting **pre-approved** means a lender reviews your financial information to estimate how much they are willing to lend you.

You can get pre-approved through:

Pre-approval shows what you CAN borrow, not what you SHOULD borrow.

- Banks
- Credit unions
- Mortgage lenders
- Online mortgage companies

During pre-approval, the lender will check your credit, income, debts, and savings. They will also give you an estimated interest rate and loan amount.

It is important to understand that **pre-approval shows what you can borrow, not what you should borrow**. Many people get into trouble by shopping at the top of their approval range instead of sticking to a healthy payment.

Pre-approval is a tool, not permission.

3. FIND A REALTOR (OPTIONAL, BUT HELPFUL)

A **realtor** helps guide you through the buying process, but **a realtor is not required** for you to purchase a home. Some buyers choose to work directly with sellers, especially in private or for-sale-by-owner situations.

When used well, a realtor can help you:

- Find homes that match your budget

- Understand market pricing
- Navigate offers and negotiations
- Avoid common mistakes
- Manage deadlines and paperwork

The most important thing is choosing someone who respects your budget and priorities. A good realtor supports discipline and does not pressure you to buy.

4. HOUSE SHOP WITHIN YOUR BUDGET

This is where emotions can take over if you are not careful.

House shopping should stay aligned with the budget you already determined, not what lenders or listings tempt you with. You should only look at homes that fit your healthy payment range and factor in all costs, not just the loan itself.

This step is about long-term sustainability. A home should support your life, not stretch it thin.

5. MAKE AN OFFER

Once you find a home that fits your budget and needs, **you or your realtor** submit an offer to the seller.

An offer includes:

- The price you are willing to pay
- Earnest money
- Timelines
- Conditions, such as inspections

The seller may accept the offer, reject it, or counter it with different terms.

Negotiation is normal. This step is not about winning. It is about protecting your financial future.

6. HOME INSPECTION

A **home inspection** evaluates the physical condition of the property.

An inspector checks major systems such as:

- Roof
- Foundation
- Electrical
- Plumbing
- HVAC

This step helps identify potential problems before you commit.

Inspections give you information and leverage. They can lead to repairs, price adjustments, or walking away if the risks are too high.

7. APPRAISAL

The **appraisal** confirms the home's value for the lender.

This protects both the bank and the buyer by ensuring the home is worth the agreed price. If the appraisal comes in lower than expected, the deal may need to be renegotiated.

This step prevents you from overpaying.

8. TITLE COMPANY

The **title company** ensures the home has clear legal ownership.

They verify there are no:

- Unpaid taxes
- Liens
- Ownership disputes

They handle the legal transfer of the property and manage funds during the transaction.

This step protects you from legal problems after purchase.

9. CLOSING

Closing is the final step, when ownership officially transfers.

At closing, you sign loan documents, pay closing costs, and receive the keys. If every previous step was handled correctly, this should feel smooth and predictable, not stressful.

You are now a homeowner!

RESPONSIBILITIES OF HOMEOWNERSHIP

Owning a home comes with responsibilities that go far beyond making a monthly payment. Unlike renting, **there is no landlord** to call when something breaks. Homeowners are responsible for ongoing maintenance, repairs, and upkeep of both the interior and exterior of the property.

This includes routine maintenance, unexpected repairs, lawn and exterior care, and long-term planning for larger expenses such as roofs, appliances, or major systems. These costs are not optional, and they rarely happen at convenient times. Because of this, emergency savings are not just helpful. They are essential. Without savings, even small repairs can quickly turn into financial stress or debt.

Homeownership rewards preparation. The more financially stable you are when you buy, the easier these responsibilities are to manage.

THE ULTIMATE GOAL: A PAID-OFF HOME

A paid-off home is one of the strongest financial positions a person can reach. When the mortgage is gone, housing costs drop dramatically, leaving only taxes, insurance, and maintenance.

This creates an enormous shift in financial freedom. Monthly expenses fall, stress decreases, and flexibility increases. In retirement, this is often the difference between simply getting by and living comfortably. For many people, retirement only works because their home is paid off.

A home that is owned outright provides security, stability, and peace of mind.

A home that is owned outright provides security, stability, and peace of mind. It turns housing from a permanent monthly obligation into a long-term asset that supports your lifestyle instead of limiting it.

PROPERTY TAXES (EVEN AFTER THE MORTGAGE IS PAID OFF)

Property taxes are an annual tax paid to your local government based on the value of your home. These taxes help fund things like schools, roads, emergency services, and local infrastructure.

Unlike a mortgage, **property taxes never go away**.

Even if you fully pay off your home and owe nothing to a bank, you are still required to pay property taxes every year for as long as you own the property. Failing to pay them can eventually result in penalties, liens, or even foreclosure by the local government.

Property taxes are usually calculated as a percentage of your home's assessed value. The exact rate depends on where you live, but it is common for homeowners to pay **thousands of dollars per year** in property taxes.

For example, a home valued at $300,000 in an area with a 1.2% property tax rate would owe approximately $3,600 per year or $300 per month in property taxes alone.

When you have a mortgage, property taxes are often included in your monthly payment and held in an escrow account. This makes them feel invisible. Once the mortgage is paid off, that same bill arrives directly, usually once or twice per year. Many homeowners are surprised by this if they have not planned for it.

This is why a paid-off home does not mean zero housing costs. It means **dramatically lower costs**, but not no costs.

WHY THIS STILL MAKES A PAID-OFF HOME POWERFUL

Even with property taxes and insurance, a paid-off home is still one of the strongest financial positions possible. While renters typically see housing costs rise over time, property taxes tend to increase more slowly and predictably.

A homeowner with a paid-off house may still pay:

- Property taxes
- Homeowners insurance
- Maintenance and repairs

But they no longer have a mortgage payment, which is usually the largest monthly expense. This reduction in fixed costs is a major reason retirement becomes more affordable for homeowners.

WHY STARTING DEBT-FREE CHANGES EVERYTHING

Starting your career with little to no debt changes the entire trajectory of homeownership. Without heavy student loans, credit card balances, or car payments, you are able to **save faster**, **qualify for better mortgage rates**, and **buy a home earlier or more comfortably**.

Lower debt means lower risk in the eyes of lenders and more flexibility in your budget. It reduces the chance of becoming house poor and increases your ability to handle repairs, emergencies, and long-term goals without panic.

Debt delays the American Dream. Discipline accelerates it. The choices you make early determine how quickly homeownership becomes a source of freedom instead of stress.

CORE TEACHING MESSAGE

A home should be a foundation for freedom, not a financial prison.

The goal is not just to buy a house.

The goal is to one day own it outright.

A healthy home purchase is decided years before you buy, based on how much debt you avoid and how much money you save.

STUDENT EXERCISE—HOME BUYING

This exercise helps students understand what it really takes to buy a home responsibly and why patience, low debt, and preparation matter more than rushing into homeownership.

PART 1: INCOME & TAKE-HOME PAY

Expected career / job: ________________________

Annual gross salary: $____________________

Estimated taxes: ☐ Use 25% rule ☐ Use known estimate

Estimated annual take-home pay: $____________________

Estimated monthly take-home pay: $____________________

PART 2: HEALTHY HOUSING TARGET

Rule: Housing should be **25–30% of take-home pay**.

Monthly take-home pay: $____________________

- 25% housing target: $____________________
- 30% housing max: $____________________

Maximum healthy monthly housing payment: $____________________

PART 3: WHAT GOES INTO A MORTGAGE PAYMENT (PITI + HOA)

Estimate realistic monthly costs.

Category	Monthly Cost
Principal & interest	$________________________
Property taxes	$________________________
Homeowners insurance	$________________________
HOA (if applicable)	$________________________
Total housing payment	$________________________

Does this fit within your healthy range? ☐ Yes ☐ No

PART 4: HOME PRICE & DOWN PAYMENT

Target home price: $_______________

Down payment percentage: ☐ 5% ☐ 10% ☐ 20% ☐ Other: _____%

Down payment amount: $__________________

Loan amount (home price – down payment): $_______________________

PART 5: MORTGAGE DETAILS

Interest rate (estimate): _______%

Loan term: ☐ 30 years ☐ 20 years ☐ 15 years

Estimated monthly principal & interest: $______________________

PART 6: REALITY CHECK (HOUSE-POOR TEST)

Answer the following questions honestly.

1. This payment would allow you to still:

☐ Save monthly ☐ Invest for retirement ☐ Handle repairs ☐ Enjoy life

2. Would a loss of income make your house payment stressful? ☐ Yes ☐ No

3. Is this house based on what you can afford now, not what you hope to earn later?

☐ Yes ☐ No

PART 7: PREPARATION PLAN

If this house is not affordable today, what needs to change?

☐ Increase down payment ☐ Reduce other debt ☐ Increase income

☐ Buy a less expensive home ☐ Delay purchase

Which change would help the most, and why?______________________________

____

____

STUDENT FINAL REFLECTION

What surprised you most about buying a home?____________________________

____

Would rushing into homeownership help or hurt you? ☐ Help ☐ Hurt

Is patience a financial advantage? ☐ Yes ☐ No

PARENT-GUIDED DISCUSSION

This discussion should focus on long-term stability, not pressure to buy quickly.

How realistic is the home price compared to income?

How does existing debt affect affordability?

What risks come with stretching your house payment?

How does saving a larger down payment change the outcome?

What does being "house poor" look like in real life?

INVESTING & RETIREMENT

HOW MONEY GROWS, WHY TIME MATTERS, AND HOW EARLY CHOICES CHANGE EVERYTHING

Up to this point, we've talked a lot about **avoiding debt** via student loans, car payments, credit cards, and overspending. Avoiding debt is critical, but it is only **half of the equation**.

The other half is learning how to **make your money work for you**.

This section is not about becoming a stock market expert. It is about understanding **how money grows** over time, why starting early matters so much, and how everyday decisions shape your future long before retirement ever feels real.

WHAT IS INVESTING?

Investing means putting money into assets that are expected to grow over time. Instead of sitting still in a checking account, invested money has the opportunity to grow, compound, and build wealth without additional work.

Common investment assets include stocks, bonds, mutual funds, and index funds. While the names may sound complicated, the concept is simple: your money is participating in long-term economic growth.

WHAT IS COMPOUND GROWTH?

Compound growth is the most important concept in investing.

It means you earn returns not only on your original money, but also on the returns that money has already earned. Over time, this creates a powerful snowball effect.

This is why **time matters more than how much you invest**.

WHY TIME MATTERS MORE THAN AMOUNT

To understand the power of time, let's compare three people who all earn the same average return but start investing at different ages.

Assume an average annual return of approximately 8%.

Person	Start Age	Monthly Investment	Total Invested	Value at Age 65
A	16	$100	~$58,800	~$450,000+
B	25	$300	~$144,000	~$430,000
C	35	$500	~$180,000	~$370,000

KEY TAKEAWAY:

The person who invested the least actual money ended up with the most, simply because they started earlier.

EXAMPLE: STARTING AT 16 YEARS OLD

Now, let's look at a real-life example. Imagine a student who starts investing at age 16 by putting away $100 per month from a part-time job. They earn an average return of 8% and continue investing until age 65.

Category	Amount
Total invested	~$58,800
Value at retirement	~$450,000–$500,000
Growth earned	~$400,000+

That is nearly half a million dollars built from a **small, consistent habit**, not a high income.

WHERE DOES THE MONEY COME FROM?

Many people believe they don't have money to invest, but in reality, their money is already committed elsewhere.

Here are common monthly payments that quietly prevent investing:

Expense	Monthly	Yearly
Car payment	$400	$4,800
Student loan	$500	$6,000
Credit card payment	$200	$2,400
Total	**$1,100**	**$13,200**

Many people believe they don't have money to invest, but in reality, their money is already committed elsewhere.

WHAT IF THAT MONEY WAS INVESTED INSTEAD?

If the same $1,100 per month were invested at an 8% average return, the long-term impact would look like this:

Time Invested	Approximate Value
10 years	~$200,000
20 years	~$650,000
30 years	~$1.6 million+

This is why "just a car payment" or "just minimum payments" matter. You're not only losing the monthly payment, but you're also losing future options.

WHAT IS RETIREMENT?

Retirement is not about age. It is about reaching a point where your investments and assets support your lifestyle.

The goal is not to stop living. Rather, it's to stop being forced to work.

HOW MUCH DO YOU NEED FOR RETIREMENT?

A common guideline is that you need about 70–80% of your working income to maintain a similar lifestyle in retirement. This assumes a paid-off home, little to no debt, and a controlled lifestyle.

Working Income	Retirement Income Target
$50,000	$35,000–$40,000
$75,000	$52,000–$60,000
$100,000	$70,000–$80,000

This gives us a yearly income goal, but the next question is the one most people never ask:

How much money do I actually need saved to produce that income?

WHAT SIZE RETIREMENT ACCOUNT SUPPORTS THAT INCOME?

A common planning rule is the **4% rule**, which suggests that you can safely withdraw about **4% of your retirement savings per year** without running out of money over the life of your retirement.

Using that guideline, here is approximately how much you would need saved at retirement and what it would take to get there with steady investing over time.

Assumptions used for illustration:

- Retirement age: 65
- Average return while investing: ~7%
- Long-term, consistent monthly investing

Retirement Income Target	Total Needed at Retirement	Approx. Monthly Investing (30–40 years)
$40,000 / year	~$1,000,000	~$350–$450 / month
$55,000 / year	~$1,375,000	~$500–$650 / month
$75,000 / year	~$1,875,000	~$700–$900 / month

WHY THIS MATTERS

These numbers may look large at first, but they become far more achievable when investing starts early. Someone who begins investing in their late teens or early twenties has decades of compounding working for them, dramatically reducing how much they need to invest each month.

Starting later means:

Turn the page to find out!

- Higher monthly investment requirements
- More pressure on income
- Fewer options

This is why **avoiding debt early** and **investing consistently** matters more than chasing high salaries later.

WHY A PAID-OFF HOME CHANGES EVERYTHING

A paid-off home eliminates the largest monthly expense most people have. Without a mortgage payment, required retirement income drops significantly, making retirement far more achievable.

For many people, retirement only works because their home is paid off.

RETIREMENT ACCOUNTS YOU'LL SEE AT WORK

- A **401(k)** is a retirement account offered through an employer. Contributions are automatically taken from your paycheck, often come with tax advantages, and may include an employer match. An employer match is essentially free money.
- A **Roth IRA** is an individual retirement account funded with after-tax money. It grows tax-free, and withdrawals in retirement are also tax-free. This makes it especially powerful for young people with long time horizons.
- A **regular brokerage account** is a standard investment account where you can buy stocks, ETFs, and other investments with no age restrictions, no contribution limits, and full access to your money anytime, but you pay taxes on dividends and gains every year. This is a good investment account to use outside of retiring and is not necessarily long term. This is a good option if

you still want to grow your money, but also take some out for other investments like homes and business opportunities. Just gives you a little more flexibility with your money and you don't have to worry about penalties if you want to withdraw money before the age of 60. But remember this account has no tax advantages and you will pay full tax on all growth.

TAX-ADVANTAGED VS. REGULAR INVESTING

Account Type	Taxes Paid Now	Taxes Paid Later
401(k)	No	Yes
Roth IRA	Yes	No
Brokerage account	Yes	Yes

Tax advantages allow more money to stay invested longer, increasing compounding and long-term growth.

WHY SO MANY PEOPLE ARE UNPREPARED

More than half of Americans have less than $100,000 saved for retirement, and nearly one in three have nothing saved at all. Many don't start until their 30s or 40s.

The issue is rarely income. The issue is lost time.

THE BIGGEST MISTAKE

Many people believe they will start later or catch up. Unfortunately, time is the one thing investing cannot replace.

You cannot make up for lost years of compounding.

CORE TEACHING MESSAGE

It's not about investing a lot of money.
It's about **starting early** and staying consistent.
Avoiding debt gives you breathing room.
Investing early gives you options.

Every dollar you don't send to debt
is a dollar working for your future.

STUDENT EXERCISE—INVESTING & RETIREMENT

This exercise connects every decision learned so far (budgeting, debt, cars, college, and housing) to the desired long-term outcome: **financial freedom in retirement**. The goal is to show how small, consistent choices made early create massive differences later in life.

PART 1: UNDERSTANDING YOUR INVESTING TIMELINE

Your current age:______________

Age you want the option to retire or be financially independent:____________________

Total years your money could grow: _______________years

Reminder: Time is the single most powerful factor in investing.

PART 2: FIRST INVESTING SCENARIO—STARTING EARLY

Scenario A: Early Start

Age started investing: _____________

Monthly investment amount: $____________

Expected average annual return: ☐ 6% ☐ 7% ☐ 8%

Years invested: _____________

Estimated total amount invested: $____________________

Estimated value at retirement: $_________________

PART 3: SECOND INVESTING SCENARIO—STARTING LATER

Scenario B: Delayed Start

Age started investing: ____________

Monthly investment amount: $___________

Expected average annual return: ☐ 6% ☐ 7% ☐ 8%

Years invested: ____________

Estimated total amount invested: $____________________

Estimated value at retirement: $_________________

PART 4: COMPARE THE OUTCOMES

Which scenario invested more actual money? ☐ Scenario A ☐ Scenario B

Which scenario ended with more money? ☐ Scenario A ☐ Scenario B

Why did this happen? ____

____

____

PART 5: DEBT VS. INVESTING TRADE-OFF

Choose one monthly payment you could avoid:

☐ Car payment ☐ Student loan ☐ Credit card ☐ Other: ____________________

Monthly payment amount: $________________

If invested instead for _______________ years at ____%:

Estimated value at retirement: $______________

This is the real cost of debt.

PART 6: RETIREMENT LIFESTYLE PLANNING

Expected working salary before retirement: $____________________ per year

Target retirement income (**70–80% rule**): $_______________ – $_________per year

Do you expect to have a paid-off home in retirement? ☐ Yes ☐ No

How does a paid-off home affect how much you need?________________________

____

____

PART 7: RETIREMENT ACCOUNTS KNOWLEDGE CHECK

Match the account to its benefit:

401(k): _________________________

Roth IRA:_________________________

Taxable brokerage account: _________________________

Which account(s) give tax advantages? ☐ 401(k) ☐ Roth IRA ☐ Both

STUDENT FINAL REFLECTION

What decision you make today will most affect your future wealth?_____________

____

What surprised you most about investing?_________________________________

____

Does starting early matter more than investing large amounts later? ☐ Yes ☐ No

PARENT-GUIDED DISCUSSION

This conversation should emphasize habits and consistency, not perfection.

What surprised you most about how money grows over time?

How did starting earlier change the outcome compared to investing more later?

Which debts most prevent investing early?

How does having a paid-off home affect retirement security?

What investing habits could you realistically start now?

WANT TO MAKE SMART MOVES NOW?

Contact a CPA, financial advisors, or other money expert today to help create good financial plans for the future. This way, you h ave a team at your disposal every step along the way as you plan for your future.

BUDGETING

TURNING YOUR FUTURE LIFE VISION INTO REAL NUMBERS

To start, we are going to **dream and imagine** what life will look like once you enter your career and adulthood. Where will you live? What will your lifestyle look like? What kinds of things will you be able to afford? What will your day-to-day life actually cost?

You have already done a version of this when you mapped out your goals. Now we are going to take it a step further by putting **real numbers** behind that vision. Instead of guessing, we are going to look at what life actually costs on a **monthly basis**.

To do this, we will use current American averages for monthly expenses. These numbers may be higher or lower depending on where you live, but they give us a strong and realistic baseline for understanding the cost of everyday life. You can always adjust the numbers later based on your local area.

What we are building is a **budget**, one of the most important financial tools you will ever use. **A budget is simply a plan for where your money goes**. Unfortunately, many people never create one. When that happens, spending controls them instead of the other way around.

A 2025 financial wellness report found about **67% of U.S. workers** said they are living paycheck to paycheck. This means they need most or all of their income to cover basic expenses, leaving little or nothing extra.

Without a budget:

- Bills dictate what you can and can't do.
- Money disappears without intention.
- Saving feels impossible.
- Debt becomes easy to justify.

With a budget:

- You decide where your money goes.
- You can plan for goals instead of reacting to bills.
- You gain control instead of stress.

By walking through these expenses together, you will be able to see what adult life actually costs, how quickly money gets allocated, and why financial decisions made early in life matter so much.

Once you understand this baseline, you can:

- Adjust expenses for your own situation
- Compare different career paths
- See how debt changes everything
- Decide what lifestyle is realistic and sustainable

Let's get started by breaking down the average monthly cost of living, and then we'll customize it to fit your future.

AVERAGE MONTHLY COST OF LIVING (BASELINE BUDGET)

Housing Costs (Biggest Expense)

Rent (1-bedroom or shared housing): $1,200

Renter's insurance: $20

Housing total: $1,220

Note 1: Housing alone consumes ~33% of take-home pay.

Note 2: The above estimate is modest by today's standards.

UTILITIES & HOME SERVICES

Electric: $120

Water/sewer: $60

Gas: $70

Trash: $25

Internet: $75

Utilities total: $350

Utilities are often underestimated, but they are never optional.

COMMUNICATION & SUBSCRIPTIONS

Cell phone: $90

Streaming services (Netflix, Hulu, Spotify, etc.): $50

Cloud storage/apps: $10

Communication & subscriptions total: $150

TRANSPORTATION (SECOND LARGEST EXPENSE)

Car payment: $350

Auto insurance: $160

Gas: $180

Maintenance/oil/tires (averaged): $90

Vehicle registration/inspection (averaged): $25

Transportation total: $805

Even a "reasonable" car quietly becomes very expensive.

Even a "reasonable" car quietly becomes very expensive.

FOOD & DAILY LIVING

Groceries: $450

Eating out/coffee: $200

Food total: $650

This is not luxury dining. This is normal life, every month.

HEALTH & MEDICAL

Health insurance (employee portion): $250

Out-of-pocket medical/prescriptions: $75

Health total: $325

INSURANCE (OFTEN FORGOTTEN)

Life insurance: $30

Disability insurance: $25

Insurance total: $55

These protect income. Not having either of them is a risk.

PERSONAL & MISCELLANEOUS

Clothing/shoes: $100

Haircuts/grooming: $50

Household supplies: $60

Gifts/birthdays/holidays (averaged): $75

Personal total: $285

DEBT OBLIGATIONS (NON-STUDENT)

Credit cards/small loans: $150

SAVINGS & RETIREMENT (MINIMUM RESPONSIBLE AMOUNT)

Emergency savings: $150

Retirement (401k/IRA): $300

Savings total: $450

Many Americans skip this, which is why emergencies become disasters.

TOTAL MONTHLY EXPENSES

Housing: $1,220

Utilities: $350

Communication: $150

Transportation: $805

Food: $650

Health: $325

Insurance: $55

Personal/Misc: $285

Debt (non-student): $150

Savings / retirement: $450

TOTAL: $4,440

For this example, this individual needs to earn **$53,280 per year** to support this lifestyle based on the monthly budget we just built.

At first glance, this seems simple. If this person earns **$60,000 per year**, they should be doing very well and have plenty of extra money left over, right?

Unfortunately, that assumption ignores taxes.

TAXES: THE MISSING PIECE MOST PEOPLE FORGET

Before you can spend any of your income, a portion of it is taken out automatically. You do not get to choose whether to pay these taxes, and they come out before the money ever reaches your bank account. You have already heard all of this and this will sound redundant, but so are taxes.

Just a reminder, there are several types of taxes that apply to most workers:

- **Federal income tax**, which is taxed at different rates as your income increases
- **Social Security tax**, which helps fund retirement and disability programs
- **Medicare tax**, which helps fund healthcare for older Americans
- **State income tax**, which applies in many states

Because tax systems are complex and vary by location, we use a rule of thumb for planning purposes.

THE 25% TAX RULE (SIMPLE AND CONSERVATIVE)

A good rule of thumb when estimating taxes is to assume **25%** of your gross income will go to taxes. This is not exact, but it is intentionally conservative and works well for budgeting and financial decision-making.

In some cases, your taxes may be slightly lower. In high-tax states or those with fewer deductions, your taxes may be higher.

The purpose of this rule is not precision. It is protection. Planning with conservative assumptions prevents you from overestimating how much money you will actually have available.

APPLYING THE RULE TO THIS EXAMPLE

Gross salary: $60,000

Estimated taxes (25%): –$15,000

Estimated take-home pay: $45,000 per year

That means even though this person earns $60,000, they only have about $45,000 available to actually spend.

WHY THIS MATTERS

This is where many people get into trouble. They make financial decisions based on their salary instead of their **take-home pay**. Rent, car payments, student loans, and everyday expenses must all be paid with money that remains after taxes.

So while $60,000 sounds like enough to comfortably support a $53,280 lifestyle, once taxes are accounted for, this individual is actually short of cash before even considering emergencies, savings, or unexpected expenses.

This is why:

- Budgeting must be done using take-home pay
- Debt becomes dangerous very quickly
- Small miscalculations create big financial stress

KEY LESSON

Never plan your life using **gross income**.
Always plan using **take-home pay**.
Taxes come first, not last. Ignoring them is one of the fastest ways to feel financially behind, even with a "good" salary.

USING ACTUAL TAXES (MORE REALISTIC EXAMPLE)

For this example, instead of using the 25% rule, we are going to assume we know the actual tax amounts for this individual.

ANNUAL TAX BREAKDOWN

Tax Type	Approximate Amount
Federal income tax	$5,200
Social Security & Medicare (FICA)	$4,590
State income tax	$2,400
Total Taxes	**~$12,200**

Now let's apply this to the salary.

Gross salary: $60,000

Total taxes: –$12,200

Take-home pay: $47,800 per year

THE PROBLEM BECOMES CLEAR

Earlier, we calculated that this individual's lifestyle costs $53,280 per year. Where does this leave us with $47,800 of take-home pay?

- **Take-home pay:** $47,800
- **Annual spending:** $53,280
- **Annual shortfall:** $5,480

Uh-oh.

This person is spending **$5,480 more per year** than they actually take home. At first glance, this doesn't seem possible, but in real life, this is extremely common.

HOW DOES THIS HAPPEN?

Most often, the gap between take-home pay and lifestyle expenses is covered by:

- Credit cards
- Small personal loans
- Buy-now-pay-later services

This is likely where the $150 per month in credit card and small loan payments in the budget came from. Instead of solving the problem, these tools quietly push the individual further into trouble by adding interest, minimum payments, and long-term stress.

We will talk more about credit cards later, but for now it's important to understand this pattern.

WHAT DO MOST PEOPLE DO NEXT?

Sadly, most people don't fix the root problem. Instead, they try to survive month to month.

They look at the budget and think:

"I'll just stop saving for now. Once things get better, I'll start again."

Then they take the $450 per month they were putting toward emergency savings and retirement contributions and put it toward daily expenses. That equals $5,400 per year, which almost perfectly covers the $5,480 shortfall.

On paper the proble looks solve In reality, i not.

On paper, the problem looks solved.

In reality, it's not.

THE HIDDEN COST OF THIS DECISION

By eliminating savings and retirement contributions, this person is now:

- Living paycheck to paycheck
- One emergency away from debt
- Building no long-term security
- Missing the most powerful years of investing
- Working only to pay bills

This is one of the most common financial traps people fall into. People don't fall for it because they are irresponsible, but because they were never taught how to see the problem early. Years later, they may look back and wonder why they worked so hard but have nothing to show for it.

A BETTER QUESTION TO ASK

Instead of asking:

"How do I make this work month to month?"

The better question is:

"How do I change this so my future improves?"

LET'S FIX THE PROBLEM THE RIGHT WAY

Next, we are going to build a new budget for this individual by:

- Eliminating unnecessary debt
- Cutting unneeded or inflated spending
- Creating positive cash flow
- Protecting savings and future goals

By doing this, we can turn the same income into a very different financial future.

Let's see what that looks like.

OPTIMIZED MONTHLY BUDGET

Debt-Free, Intentional Spending, Based on $47,800 Take-Home Pay

Assumptions

- Annual take-home pay: $47,800
- Monthly take-home pay: $3,983
- No student loans
- No credit card debt
- No car payment
- Modest lifestyle
- Priority: Avoid debt, build savings, invest early

HOUSING (CONTROLLED)

Rent (roommate or modest unit): $900

Renter's insurance: $15

Housing total: $915

UTILITIES & HOME SERVICES

Electric: $90

Water/sewer: $45

Gas: $55

Trash: $20

Internet: $60

Utilities total: $270

COMMUNICATION

Cell phone (budget carrier): $50

Streaming (1–2 services): $25

Communication total: $75

TRANSPORTATION (NO CAR PAYMENT)

Auto insurance: $120

Gas: $150

Maintenance/repairs (averaged): $80

Registration/inspection (averaged): $20

Transportation total: $370

FOOD

Groceries: $425

Eating out/coffee: $100

Food total: $525

HEALTH & MEDICAL

Health insurance (employee portion): $250

Prescriptions/co-pays: $50

Health total: $300

INSURANCE (INCOME PROTECTION)

Life insurance: $25

Disability insurance: $25

Insurance total: $50

PERSONAL & LIFESTYLE

Clothing/shoes: $60

Haircuts/grooming: $40

Household supplies: $50

Gifts/holidays (averaged): $50

Personal total: $200

Savings & Investing (Realistic & Sustainable)

Emergency savings: $250

Retirement investing: $600

Savings total: $850

Savings are important, but only after the budget works.

TOTAL MONTHLY BUDGET

Housing: $915

Utilities: $270

Communication: $75

Transportation: $370

Food: $525

Health: $300

Insurance: $50

Personal: $200

Savings & investing: $850

TOTAL EXPENSES: $3,555

MONTHLY BUDGET COMPARISON

Category	Old Budget (Debt & Overspending)	New Budget (Debt-Free & Controlled)	What Changed
Housing	$1,220	$915	Downsized / roommate / better choice
Utilities	$350	$270	More efficient, fewer extras
Phone & subscriptions	$150	$75	Cut unused services
Transportation	$805	$370	Paid-off car, lower insurance
Food	$650	$525	Meal planning, less eating out
Health	$325	$300	Minor adjustments
Insurance (life/ disability)	$55	$50	Optimized
Personal / misc	$285	$200	Reduced impulse spending
Credit cards / small loans	$150	$0	Eliminated debt
Savings & retirement	$450	$850	Protected & increased
TOTAL MONTHLY EXPENSES	**$4,440**	**$3,555**	**Reduced expenses by $885**

MONTHLY CASH FLOW COMPARISON

	Old Budget	New Budget
Monthly take-home pay	$3,983	$3,983
Monthly expenses	$4,440	$3,555
Monthly result	**–$457**	**+ $428**

ANNUAL IMPACT

	Old Budget	New Budget
Annual shortfall / surplus	**–$5,480**	**+ $5,136**
Savings & retirement	$0 (cut to survive)	$10,200/year
Debt trend	Increasing	Decreasing
Stress level	High	Manageable
Financial control	Bills control you	You control money

WHAT THIS COMPARISON SHOWS CLEARLY

1. The Original Budget Was Broken, Even With a "Good" Salary

This person was spending more than they made before saving or investing. The gap was hidden by credit cards and small loans.

2. Cutting Savings Was NOT the Solution

Eliminating $450 per month in savings only masked the problem. It created paycheck-to-paycheck living and destroyed long-term progress.

3. The New Budget Fixes the Root Problem

The improvement came from intentional structural changes:

By addressing the causes:

- Eliminating debt
- Reducing the biggest expense categories
- Making intentional trade-offs

The result is a completely different outcome:

- Positive cash flow
- Real savings
- Less stress
- A positive, more secure financial future

FINAL CASH FLOW SNAPSHOT

Monthly Take-Home Pay: $3,983

Monthly Expenses: $3,555

Remaining Surplus: $428 per month

This surplus can be used intentionally for:

- Extra savings
- Investing more later
- Travel
- A buffer for unexpected costs
- Accelerating personal goals

WHY THIS MATTERS

By fixing the budget structure, retirement and savings contributions more than doubled, putting over **$10,000** per year toward the future while still leaving $428 left over every month to use by choice, not necessity.

This means the budget didn't just break even.

It effectively **increased usable income and savings by $15,336 per year**.

Compare that to the original situation, where overspending was "solved" by completely eliminating savings and retirement, leaving nothing to show for years of work.

The budget didn't just break even. It increased usable income and savings by $15,336 per year.

THINK BIGGER THAN THE MONTHLY NUMBER

Now imagine what an extra $500 per month actually provides:

- A vacation without credit cards
- A growing emergency fund
- Increased retirement and investment contributions
- A financial buffer for unexpected expenses

The power of budgeting is that you aren't forced you to choose just one of the above.

When your money is under control, **you can do all of them at the same time**.

WHAT BUDGETING REALLY GIVES YOU

Budgeting doesn't restrict your life.
It gives you **options, flexibility, and peace of mind**.

THE MOST IMPORTANT LESSON FOR STUDENTS

"You don't fix a broken budget by sacrificing your future.
You fix it by changing the decisions that broke it."

WHY THIS MATTERS LONG-TERM

If this new budget is followed consistently:

- Savings compound
- Emergencies don't cause panic
- Career flexibility increases
- Wealth becomes possible

All without earning more money.

This brings us to **one of the most important lessons** in this entire curriculum:

More money does not solve spending problems.

You can earn six figures, seven figures, or even tens of millions of dollars and still end up broke if your spending grows faster than your income. Income alone does not create financial security. Structure does.

That is why having a system in place is critical. A system allows you to:

- Know exactly where every dollar is going
- Make intentional choices instead of emotional ones
- Prevent small problems from becoming big ones
- Build consistency regardless of income level

Without a system, money disappears. Bills pile up. Stress increases. And people are left wondering where their income went.

This is why we ended this curriculum with budgeting. Budgeting is arguably the most important financial skill you can learn because it connects everything else:

- Career choices
- Lifestyle decisions
- Debt management
- Saving and investing
- Long-term goals

A budget is not about restriction. It is about control.

You either control your money, or your money will control you.

Once you understand and apply budgeting, every other financial concept in this curriculum becomes easier, clearer, and more effective.

FINAL REAL-LIFE BUDGET & FINANCIAL PLAN

END-OF-CURRICULUM CAPSTONE WORKSHEET

This worksheet is the final step of the curriculum. It brings together every lesson learned: career choice, education cost, taxes, budgeting, debt, cars, housing, investing, and retirement.

The goal is simple but powerful. It aims to answer one question:

Can the life you imagined at the beginning actually work in the real world?

This is not about perfection. It is about awareness, trade-offs, and intentional decisions. Feel free to use every resource at your disposal to get real-life estimates. Find a house you want to buy or a place you would like to rent. You can go through this exercise several times and paint many different scenarios. Parents can share their real-life scenarios as well.

PART 1: CAREER & INCOME REALITY

Chosen career/job: ________________________________

Expected starting salary (gross): $____________________ per year

Estimated taxes: ☐ Use actual estimate ☐ Use 25% rule

Estimated annual take-home pay: $____________________

Estimated monthly take-home pay: $____________________

PART 2: EDUCATION & DEBT SUMMARY

Type of education completed: ☐ Community college ☐ Trade/technical school ☐ 4-year college ☐ Graduate school ☐ Other:____________________

Total education cost: $______________

Scholarships/grants: –$______________

Family contribution: –$______________

Total student loan debt: $______________

Estimated monthly student loan payment: $______________

Does this follow the salary-to-debt rules? ☐ Yes ☐ No

PART 3: HOUSING BUDGET

Housing type: ☐ Rent ☐ Own ☐ Living with family

Housing Costs Monthly

Rent/mortgage: $______________

Property taxes: $__________

Insurance: $____________

HOA (if any): $__________

Utilities: $__________

Total housing cost: $__________

Does this stay within 25–30% of take-home pay? ☐ Yes ☐ No

PART 4: TRANSPORTATION

Transportation Costs Monthly

Car payment: $______________

Auto insurance: $__________________

Gas: $________________

Maintenance: $______________

Total transportation: $_____________

Does this feel manageable? ☐ Yes ☐ No

PART 5: LIVING EXPENSES

Living Expenses Monthly

Food (groceries + eating out): $__________________

Phone/internet: $__________________

Health insurance/medical: $_______________

Personal/entertainment: $_________________

Miscellaneous: $_____________

Total living expenses: $__________________

PART 6: DEBT PAYMENTS (NON-EDUCATION)

Debt Payments Monthly

Credit cards: $_______________

Personal loans: $__________________

Other debt: $________________

Total non-education debt: $______________

PART 7: SAVINGS & INVESTING PLAN

Savings Monthly

Emergency fund: $________________

Retirement (401k/Roth IRA): $____________

Other investing: $_________________

Total savings & investing: $_____________

PART 8: MONTHLY BUDGET SUMMARY

Monthly take-home pay: $_________________

Total monthly expenses: $_________________

Monthly surplus / shortfall: $_______________

☐ Budget is positive ☐ Budget is negative

PART 9: REALITY CHECK & ADJUSTMENTS

If your budget is negative, what needs to change? (Check all that apply)

☐ Lower housing cost ☐ Reduce car cost ☐ Reduce education debt

☐ Cut discretionary spending ☐ Delay purchases ☐ Increase income

Which change would have the biggest impact?________________________________

____

____

____

PART 10: DREAM VS. REALITY REFLECTION

Return to your Life Goals & Vision Worksheet and answer the following questions:

Which goals are fully supported by this budget?____________________

____

Which goals require changes or patience?____________________

____

What surprised you most when comparing dreams to reality?____________________

____

____

____

STUDENT FINAL TAKEAWAY

What is the most important financial rule you learned?____________________

____

What decision will matter most for your future?____________________

____

Do you now feel more confident about real-life money decisions? ☐ Yes ☐ No

PARENT-GUIDED DISCUSSION

This final discussion should focus on growth, awareness, and confidence, not criticism.

How realistic is this budget compared to initial goals?

Where did debt have the biggest impact?

What decisions created the most flexibility?

How does this budget change long-term outcomes?

What habits matter more than exact numbers?

IN CLOSING

I hope this exercise motivates you to move toward your goals and doesn't discourage you from them. The purpose of this curriculum is not to tell you what you *can't* do, but to show you how to put yourself in the strongest possible position when adult life begins.

You can absolutely reach the goals you've written down. The key is how you start. Don't begin life in a hole. Starting with less debt, smarter choices, and a clear plan gives you options, something many people never have.

You can still buy the car you want. You can still own a home you're proud of. And the truth is, you don't need to make a crazy amount of money to do it. You just need to make smart decisions early, avoid unnecessary debt, and invest your money now so you can enjoy it later.

Remember this: It doesn't matter how much money you make if you make poor financial decisions. People with high incomes still go broke. They still live stressed, paycheck-to-paycheck lives. Income alone does not create freedom. Decisions do.

Be a good steward of your money. When you manage it with intention, discipline, and patience, you'll be surprised by the opportunities, stability, and freedom that follow.

This is how you build a real life on purpose.

Make smart decisions early, avoid unnecessary debt, and invest your money now so you can enjoy it later.

Real-Life Money Cheat Sheet

Formulas & Quick References

Mortgage Payments

$$\text{Monthly Payment} = P \times \left[\frac{r(1+r)^n}{(1+r)^n - 1} \right]$$

P = Loan Amount

R = Monthly Interest Rate

N = Number of Payments

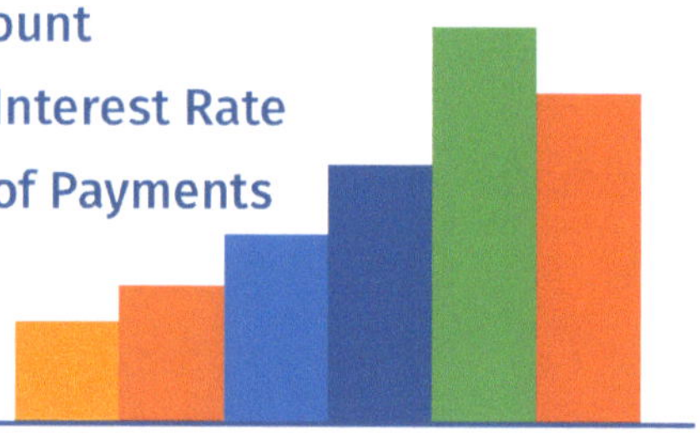

Even after a home is paid off, you still owe property taxes every year.

Credit Card Payments

Monthly Interest = Balance x (APR + 12)

Minimum Payments = Maximum Cost

Student Loans

$$\text{Monthly Payment} = P \times \left[\frac{r(1+r)^n}{(1+r)^n - 1} \right]$$

Standard Plan	10 Years	20-25 Years
Lower Payment		Lower Payment
Income-Driven		More Interest

Credit Score Guide

- Payment History
- Credit Utilization
- Length of Credit
- Account Mgmt.

A Good Score = Better Rates & More Apporval

Time vs. Money

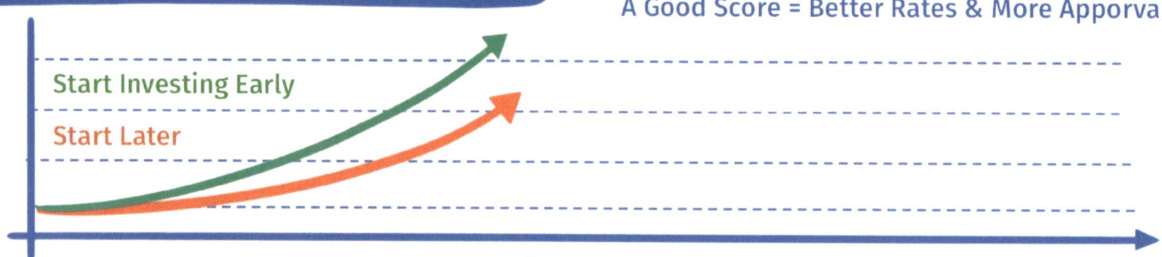

Starting Young = Bigger Future!

"Know the Rules, Win the Game!"

Real-Life Money Cheat Sheet

Smart Strategies for Major Purchases

Buying a Home

30 - Year Option

30 Year

< 25%

Of take-home pay

- < 25% of take-home pay
- 8-10% minimum down payment
- Lower monthly payment

15 - Year Option

15 Year

< 25%

Of take-home pay

Much Less Interest Paid

- < 25% of take-home pay
- At least 20% down
- Home paid off sooner

Being able to afford a 15-year mortgage shows you are in a stronger position to buy a home and sets you up for a better future.

Buying a Car

Recommended Income Rule: <10% of take-home pay on a car

- Save first, then buy
- Total vehicle cost < half your income
- Payment <10% of take-home pay

$24,000
Monthly Payment
$500

Car payments keep people in debt cycle-they prevent investing

Choosing a College

Recommended Income Rule: <75% of anticipated starting salary

- Seek scholarships & financial aid
- Choose a college you can afford, no matter the name
- College is not the only option!

Trade schools, certifications, and other careers can be just as lucrative.

$LOAN
$ 35,000
Monthly Payment. $350+

"Where You Go Sets Up Where You End up."

Index

Symbols

401(k) 92, 93, 97

A

Appraisal 78

APR 25, 26, 32, 41, 47

B

Budget 18, 26, 33, 48, 77, 101, 110, 113, 114, 115, 119, 120, 122

C

Career 5, 6, 8, 30, 51, 58, 61, 62, 65, 69, 70, 82, 83, 99, 100, 119

Car poor 35, 36

Cars 22, 36, 37, 39, 40, 43, 45, 46, 54, 71, 95, 119

Closing 79

Compound growth 88

Compounding 45, 57, 91, 93

Credit cards 22, 24, 27, 28, 30, 33, 34, 36, 54, 72, 73, 87, 108, 115, 117

D

Debt 5, 6, 13, 18, 22, 24, 25, 27, 30, 31, 34, 36, 37, 39, 40, 42, 52, 53, 54, 55, 58, 59, 60, 61, 62, 63, 64, 67, 68, 69, 70, 72, 73, 75, 79, 82, 83, 85, 86, 87, 90, 92, 94, 95, 96, 100, 109, 110, 114, 115, 119, 120, 121, 122, 124, 125

Debt ceilings 61, 64

Debt goals 61, 64

Depreciating asset 37

Depreciation 37, 43, 44

Down payment 45, 74, 75, 84, 85, 86

E

Education 9, 61, 120, 121

Equity 38, 72

G

Golden handcuffs 58

Gross pay 12, 13

H

HOA fees 72, 75, 76

Home inspection 78

I

Income-to-debt ratio 54

Insurance 5, 30, 43, 45, 63, 71, 74, 75, 76, 80, 81, 84, 101, 102, 110, 111, 112, 114, 121

Interest 5, 6, 8, 22, 23, 25, 26, 28, 29, 30, 32, 34, 36, 37, 39, 41, 42, 43, 44, 45, 52, 56, 57, 64, 65, 68, 70, 71, 73, 74, 75, 76, 84, 108

Interest rate 36, 70, 73, 76

Investing 26, 33, 48, 54, 87, 91, 93, 94, 95, 96, 112, 116, 122

M

Mortgage 70, 71, 72, 74, 76, 80, 81, 82, 92, 120

P

Pre-approval 76

Principal 53, 71, 84

Property taxes 80, 81

R

Regular brokerage account 92

Repayment plan 53

Roth IRA 92, 93, 97, 122

S

Salary 8, 12, 16, 18, 20, 30, 48, 52, 54, 55, 56, 58, 59, 61, 64, 65, 67, 69, 75, 83, 97, 105, 106, 107, 119, 120

Student loan 5, 52, 55, 63, 67, 120

T

Take-home pay 12, 13, 18, 20, 21, 33, 48, 56, 72, 75, 76, 83, 101, 105, 106, 107, 108, 110, 114, 119, 120, 122

Tax brackets 6, 12, 14, 15

Taxes 5, 12, 14, 16, 18, 19, 20, 21, 53, 71, 72, 75, 76, 78, 80, 81, 83, 84, 92, 104, 105, 107, 119, 120

Title company 78

Transportation 9, 47, 55, 102, 103, 111, 113, 114, 121

W

W-2 6, 12, 16, 18

Withholding 13

www.ingramcontent.com/pod-product-compliance
Lightning Source LLC
LaVergne TN
LVHW071241210926
848486LV00007B/319